MY FIGHT

MACANTHONY**MEDIA**

MY FIGHT WITH LIFE

By Leon McKenzie

Published by MacAnthony Media LTD
www.macanthonymedia.co.uk

A CIP catalogue record for this book is available from the British
Library.
ISBN 978-0-9574671-0-1

Cover design by James Oliver
Front Cover Image by Terry Harris
Back Cover Image from [PA]

Prepared by:
MacAnthony Media LTD
16 Priestgate
Peterborough
Cambridgeshire PE1 1JA
Tel: 01733 358462
Website: www.macanthonymedia.co.uk

Printed and bound by:
CPI Group (UK) Ltd,
Croydon
CR0 4YY

To my Champ, Princess, Sweetpea and Baby T.
"You are all so beautiful and bring me so much joy.
With all the highs that come with the lows I never want you to
give up.
Each one of you is so precious and so special, and I love you all
more than life itself.
Thank you for giving me a purpose to succeed, just remember
that when one dream ends another can start and come true."
I love you.
Daddy.

CONTENTS

Foreword	9
Introduction	14
It Didn't Work	18
Breaking Down Physically and Mentally	26
The Keys To Norwich	38
Warrant For My Arrest	57
I Wanted To Knock This Manager Out	68
Rage Against The System	80
Charles Bronson And Myra Hindley	88
Organised Kaos	102
Prince Of The Palace	113
God Help Me	129
Posh And Proud	139
Women Have Been My Downfall	151
The Champs	163
Father's Pride	176
Highs And Lows	183
Future Dreams	204
Don't Go Down My Path	210
Angels	217
Nearest and Dearest	223

FOREWORD

By Clarke Carlisle
Chairman
Professional Footballers Association.

The first time I met Leon in a non-football environment it wasn't exactly the scenario that would usually forge the beginnings of a strong relationship.

The corridors of the magistrates court isn't a common social meeting place, nor is it one where casual chat abounds, but it was here where we first embraced, and little chat was needed.

I'll come back to this point because the first time that I actually crossed paths with Leon was way back in 2003.

He was at Peterborough United and earning all the rave reviews that a player at the top of his game should.

Strong, quick and a natural eye for goal, he was Division Two's hot property and we at Queens Park Rangers were to be his next victims!

I was spared the ominous task of keeping him in check (by that I mean I was dropped!) and I had to watch from the bench as Steve Palmer and Terrell Forbes struggled to keep him at bay.

Goodness knows how they did, but we escaped relatively

...est London with a 0-0 draw, but ... e of Leon's form.

...other game, it wasn't long before he was ... by a Premier League club, and he got his break at ...orwich City.

To me, and I'm sure to the majority of others, here was a guy who was living the dream.

I saw what a talented player he was and wished him every success, but I didn't have a clue what was going on behind the facade.

I knew nothing of Leon's plight until he actually called me one day for help. We spoke on the phone for hours, over a couple of calls, and Leon opened up to me.

I was blown away by his honesty about what he'd been through, about the lows that he'd suffered and the extreme actions that he'd taken.

As someone who has been through the horrors of addiction and depression, I know how difficult it is to open up your soul to someone, to lay yourself bare and admit all your fears, perceived weaknesses and flaws, and how tough it is to ask for help.

In our industry it is engrained within you that fear is weakness, that men deal with things and those who don't are cast aside.

Confronting this by yourself is hard enough, but sharing it with another had been, until recent years, professional suicide!

Although Leon's circumstances were completely different to mine, his thoughts and feelings were almost identical to when I was at my lowest. I could empathize with where he had been, where he was at and where he wanted to go, and I wanted to help him in any way possible.

And so, back to our meeting at the courthouse.

I met a man at his most vulnerable. His liberty was at stake due to the illogical decisions he made whilst at the depth of his depression.

He was at the mercy of a judge who may not put a speck of credence of the destructive power of mental illness.

I wanted to give a reference for Leon at court for two reasons. The first was to try and convey what depression is... your judgment. This was by no means an 'excuse' to... Leon of any accountability for his actions, as he and I both kn... that we must bear the consequences of the choices we make.

It was, however, an attempt to explain how the decisions you make when suffering from depression are warped at best, and not the decisions that you would make when of sound mind.

By way of example, death and/or suicide seem like such viable options when you are considering a solution to the simplest of problems.

Leon will speak of his experiences in this area and if you asked him now, he'd be horrified even at the thought of going this way, but once upon a time it felt like the answer.

The second reason was because of what Leon had done since emerging from depression.

He had shown the actions of a remorseful man, of someone who wanted to make amends for all he'd done.

I saw what he was doing on a personal level, to maintain his own progress as a man and a father, and I saw what he wanted to do on a professional level, so that he could help others to benefit from his experience.

There was a fire in his belly about the whole issue of depression and mental health, and I saw a kindred spirit in this battle to help minds and to change attitudes.

When Leon was sent to prison, my heart sank. His barrister tried to tell us that the brevity of the sentence was a relative success, but it wasn't one that I could celebrate.

Seeing a man taken away from his family is a gut-wrenching scenario.

I really feared for Leon whilst he was inside. I don't know whether or not I would be able to cope were I in his position.

Being isolated for so long is a recipe for disaster when someone is a depressive. I was also worried about Leon's family.

I met his wife Sofia for the first time outside court too. I wondered how she would cope with their young children, having their father

_i positive woman. Offers of help were
take_ _ positivity shone through, and I'm sure that Leon
benefitted from that. The visiting sessions in prison were sparse and restricted numbers-wise, so I could only write to Leon while he was inside. I wanted to give him words of encouragement and pass on the good wishes that were coming from the football community.

I didn't expect a response, but I was delighted when I received it. My delight was at the words I read.

They were from a man who was up against it. He had his back to the wall but, instead of capitulating like we have in the past, he was forging plans and strategies for the future.

Ways to support his family, ways to support fellow depression sufferers and ways to support himself were dominating his thoughts.

There wasn't any bravado about him either. He was honest about how tough it was, about the thoughts that were troubling him, but he was positive about how he was going to beat them.

On coming out of prison, Leon has done even more to show me that my opinion of him was rightly held.

He has devoted himself to the Elite Welfare Management initiative in an attempt to provide a facility for our industry that will ensure that people get the help that they need.

His passion and enthusiasm for the cause is plain for all to see and he is a fantastic figurehead.

One of the strongest aids to anyone who is baring their soul is an empathetic ear, and who can offer more empathy to footballers than Leon? He has played all levels of football, achieved all manners of success, but he has also tasted all manners of trials and tribulations.

He is a generous, loving and compassionate man whose story will move you, or at the very least, make you sit up and take notice.

I am proud to know Leon, and I'm even prouder to call him my friend.

Clarke Carlisle has played football professionally for Blackpool, Queens Park Rangers, Leeds United, Watford, Luton Town, Burnley, Preston North End and Northampton Town. He is currently with League Two side York City.

Clarke has had well publicised battles with depression and alcoholism during his career, but he is now the highly-respected chairman of the management committee of the Professional Footballers Association.

Clarke's reputation as an intelligent, forthright spokesman on the issues confronting professional footballers has soared in recent times.
He has also won a competition to find Britain's brainiest footballer and he has won two episodes of cult TV show Countdown!

INTRODUCTION

Three years ago professional footballer Leon McKenzie tried to kill himself in a modest hotel room on a bleak Tuesday afternoon in Bexleyheath, Kent.

He was a handful of sleeping pills and a few minutes away from succeeding.

How did it come to this? The answer lies within the mental maelstrom that is depression.

Leon had played Premier League football and earned the wages that came with the status. He had enjoyed the trappings of fame: the women, the fast cars, the adulation of thousands of fans cheering his every move and he'd claimed over 100 goals in a career that involved eight different full-time professional clubs.

He had a loving wife and he was a devoted dad to three beautiful children and yet he felt empty, unfulfilled and scared about the future as injuries hastened the end of his football career.

This is no ordinary account of a footballer with a huge ego and a misguided belief that the public want to share the details of a perfect lifestyle played out in mansions and involving luxury holidays and star-studded parties. This is not a name-dropping tale of a boastful man.

Instead, Leon delivers a frank and harrowing account of the

stresses and pressures of sport at the highest level and of his slump into the deep depression that almost claimed his life.

On the surface, Leon had everything, but in his head he had nothing. The build-up to his suicide attempt, the act itself and the aftermath are explained in a brutally honest fashion.

Events that would seem trivial to most of us are dangerous triggers to those caught in the grip of such a serious sickness.

Leon briefly surrendered to the pressure, but he has shown that personal courage, determination and the love of a powerful unit of family and friends can pull a man back up from the depths of despair.

Even after his suicide attempt, life threw massive challenges at Leon, most notably a long, drawn-out prosecution over a handful of speeding tickets which ultimately led to a prison sentence and three months spent languishing in one of the country's toughest jails, one that housed some of the UK's most notorious killers.

Most of these words were written by Leon during his spell in Woodhill prison, a Category A facility, as long, lonely nights were spent completing a diary.

Leon grew up in a boxing family which included World, European and British Champions. He spent time in the gym himself and picked up the fighting skills that would prove useful at school, when his family name effectively placed a target on his back for young bullies, and in prison where bare-knuckle confrontations took place on a daily basis.

He also picked up from his dad, three-time British boxing champion Clinton McKenzie, first-hand knowledge of the dedication and effort required to be a high-class athlete and he used it to realise a dream of becoming a professional footballer.

His career was almost over before it started as he struggled to find a club to take him on as a youth team player, until his local club Crystal Palace gave in to teenage perseverance and offered him a trial that lasted six full months.

Once winning an Academy contract Leon's progress was rapid and, after scoring on his first-team debut as a 17 year-old, he was playing in the Premier League within two years.

After leaving Palace under a cloud, he went on to represent Fulham, Peterborough, Norwich, Coventry, Charlton, Northampton and Kettering. He is now playing non-league football for Corby Town so he has seen the highs and lows that can make up the life of a professional footballer.

He helped Norwich into the Premier League and started to earn the big money footballers expected when performing in the top flight of English football.

But he also witnessed young players going unpaid as their club simply ran out of money.

He played against some of the game's biggest stars and performed on the game's biggest stages. He has been influenced by some of football's most famous stars.

He's seen violence, humour and camaraderie in football. He was also a victim of racism.

Leon was happiest when giving pleasure to his supporters by virtue of his on-field displays, but off-the-field events were soon eating away at his well-being.

After some horrible personal battles with his first wife and with his own mind, he almost became a fatal victim of depression, a taboo subject within football at the time, but now a hot topic thanks to the candour and courage of people like Leon.

Leon leaves nothing out of his story. He's experienced some wonderful personal highs as well as the demoralising lows.

He rages against those who did him wrong. He is no supporter of the UK justice system or those with power in football who still appear reluctant to recognise and then help players with mental health issues. The courts, senior police officers and the prison system have all angered him on this journey.

But that passion is also seen in a positive light as Leon salutes the friends and colleagues who have aided what has been a remarkable recovery

He speaks openly and without embarrassment about his fight against depression, a battle he is now winning thanks to the love and support of wife Sofia, and, now, four children Kasey, Mariya, Naima and Talia, as well as his parents and close friends.

Leon wants his story to be both a warning and an education to those coming into football. The glory doesn't last forever and there will inevitably be setbacks along the way, but even if you touch rock bottom as Leon did, you should never give up hope.

Personally Leon is over the worst now and he's embarked on other potentially high-profile careers in music and in boxing, but, most importantly, he is to spend much of his time working with other footballers who are facing up to similar struggles to his.

For Leon life was almost over, but now he feels like it's just beginning again.

Alan Swann

CHAPTER 1

'IT DIDN'T WORK THEN'

I wanted to kill myself.

I'd had enough of life, my life at least, so it was time to end it all. Thoughts of suicide had popped in and out of my head for a while now, but for the last week they'd been pretty much permanent visitors.

A pulled hamstring towards the end of a training session pushed me over the edge. It was a relatively trivial moment for sure, and an occupational hazard for a footballer, but I'd been beating myself up mentally for months and this was the punch that knocked me down and out.

I could think of only one way to escape the misery that had enveloped my life. At that horrible time I couldn't explain why I felt numb, empty and desolate. On the outside I had everything, but inside I was lost in a fog of uncertainty.

I knew deep down that suicide was selfish. I knew it would cause misery and desperation to the people I loved the most and I know now that's what depression does to you.

You don't think straight. Hope is abandoned. Back then logic and rational thought had left my head months before leaving just one idea swimming back and forth inside my mind.

I wanted out. No ifs, no buts, no maybes, I wanted out and I wanted out today.

I was a man with a beautiful, loving wife and three young children who meant the world to me. They were my life and yet I wanted to leave them behind to try and find a better place for me.

They'd be better off without me anyway. I wasn't contributing much. I didn't want my sadness to crush them.

Inexplicable thoughts (although they seemed perfectly sensible at the time) like that were running through my head day after miserable, stinking day. I was trapped in a maze of mood swings that made little sense.

I'd lost sight of what was good and positive in my life. I saw only misery and uncertainty ahead.

The people I worked with didn't suspect a thing. I appeared normal to them. I would appear calm, in good humour, one of the lads, someone without a care in the world.

That was how it was in the world of professional football. You had to keep up appearances, join in the banter as most people at that time, in this macho, testosterone-filled world would view mental illness as a weakness rather than a problem that needed attention, a problem that demanded help.

I was good at keeping up appearances. I could be a livewire in the dressing room, laughing, shouting and bantering as loudly as anyone.

Inside I was dying though and I was gradually convincing myself that suicide was the best way to escape the torment.

I was a footballer at Charlton Athletic coming to the end of a career that had included two spells in the Premier League, an appearance at Wembley, a couple of promotions and some memorable and magical moments.

But I wasn't really a footballer any more as I was permanently injured and couldn't string two games together for my latest club. People, fans especially, would still envy my lifestyle. They'd assume I was collecting a few grand a week and living comfortably for doing very little, but I hated my existence.

For as long as I could remember, or at least from the time that I chose football over the family tradition of boxing, I just wanted to score goals, I wanted to play at the highest level, I wanted to be loved.

I'd achieved it all, but now it had been taken away from me by a body struggling to the point of collapse with the demands of my work. That had led to my mind falling apart as well. Now I just couldn't face the future.

After signing me, Charlton had put me up in a Marriott Hotel in Bexleyheath. I'd been there for four months, returning to an empty room after training in the early hours of the afternoon, collecting my room key, making sure the door was locked behind me, pulling the curtains, lying on the bed and either staring into space or just bursting into tears, usually the latter, often both.

I had no energy, no drive. All through my football career I'd flogged myself to the limits in training and on the pitch, and I generally lived a hectic life, but now I couldn't even be bothered to switch the TV on in my room, or make a drink, or visit the bathroom.

The sheer weight of this illness is hard to explain to those who have never come into contact with it.

I wasn't mad. I didn't feel like I'd gone crazy and there was no chance of me making trouble for anyone. I didn't have the passion that would make me rant and rave or to fight with anyone. My head was empty apart from that persistent thought of suicide.

The complete listlessness I felt when not actually playing football was so confusing. On the rare occasions that I was fit, I would still run around the training field, but I was in company then and therefore had motivation.

On the drive back to the hotel, the rot would set in. It was a familiar pattern. I was alone and there was nothing to look forward to except the darkness of my room. I hated myself and my life.

Some sufferers of depression never get to the suicide stage. I seemed to arrive there quickly. Anxiety had used up most of my energy, and all of my fight.

I certainly didn't want to be with anyone on those miserable afternoons. I had no idea what the Charlton players did after lunch because I didn't mix with them once the chore of training had been completed.

Sofia, my wife, would call. She was living in the family home with our daughter in Northampton. I'd answer, but I wasn't really there. I knew how hard I'd worked to make myself a Premier League footballer and now I was feeling desperately sorry for myself because my entire career was coming to an end.

Football had been my release from all the pressures on the outside and now football was being taken away from me. At the very moment you score against the top teams as I did, you feel invincible, but when you can't even score in five-a-side matches in training, the lows are just as extreme.

No-one had prepared me for the end of my playing days. As my career had taken off, it was all big promises of fame and massive earnings. I was surrounded by sycophants and well wishers telling me nothing could go wrong now I'd made it to the big time. I was set up for life.

That side of the game was easy to deal with. The highs provided huge rushes of adrenaline, but now those days were over the lows were proving just as extreme.

I wasn't prepared for the reality of a career collapsing in a heap, the prospect of future obscurity , and God only knows what else. This was tough and, in my head at least, I was dealing with it all on my own.

I was sick of players, coaching staff and fans staring at me. I knew what they were thinking: 'look at Leon, he's injured and not able to play again.'

After leaving Coventry to join Charlton, I'd also got myself into serious debt which obviously didn't help my state of mind so now was the time to act.

It was an unremarkable Tuesday morning when I finally decided to put my suicide plan into operation. I was training well, I felt fit for a change and then my hamstring went.

I pulled up. I couldn't run anymore. I was jinxed so what was the point in carrying on, in football or in life.

I could sense everyone glaring at me. There was sympathy from people at the club, but not everyone, and to be fair I felt embarrassed and guilty myself.

I was embarrassed because I was desperate to show this club how good I could be. Instead my body was breaking down and I was crying inside.

I went to the medical room for treatment. It was a path I knew well. I was on my own in there for a while and I just sat there on a treatment bed and roared my eyes out.

While I was there, I casually asked the club doctor for some sleeping pills, explaining that I was having too many restless nights and I was struggling to get through training as a result.

He gave me a batch to help me but like the rest of the club staff, he had no idea that what I was really suffering was a lot worse than a bout of insomnia. He also couldn't have known that I already had a separate batch of 20 sleeping pills back at the hotel.

I had enough now to be sure of making my exit. I also had some anti-inflammatories and there was an unopened bottle of Jack Daniels in my hotel room to wash everything down.

Nothing could stop me now. I drove to the hotel car park and rang my mum. I burst into tears, telling her that I couldn't take any more pain, any more anguish. I was sick of being injured and scared about what the future held for me.

Mum started crying. She hated how unhappy I had become. She hated the fact that injuries had started to interrupt my career on a regular basis and she now decided she wanted me to give up playing.

Good old mum- always practical, always caring- but she hadn't grasped what I was planning.

I fooled myself that the mental struggles I was experiencing ran deeper than a career that was coming to an inglorious end.

I tried to convince myself that I had nothing left to prove or achieve anyway. I'd found and married my soul-mate, I'd played football at the highest level, I'd scored 100 goals, I'd fathered three beautiful children.

What else was there? Especially as my body had now given way. Those glory days wouldn't be returning. My life had peaked too early and I just didn't fancy seeing out the rest of my days feeling as lost as I did at the point. I wanted those adrenaline rushes to continue.

I look back at those days now and cringe. I realise now that my 'Queen B', my name for Sofia, and my children were reason enough to keep going, but I must have been in a bad, dark place that particular night, a place I wouldn't wish on my worst enemy. I decided the world was now horrible and unforgiving and I'd seen enough of it. I wanted to join my sister Tracey who had taken her own life aged 23 eight years earlier.

Tracey wasn't my biological sister, but we were closer than most siblings. We were close enough for her to call me in tears to complain about an identity crisis as she felt unable to fit in with her white friends or her black friends (she had skin a little lighter than mine) and she was all 'messed up' as a result.

Of course, I told her what every close friend or big brother would have told her. 'Don't worry, it will be fine, I'll get down and see you soon', and I meant it.

Two days later, mum was in tears as she rang to tell me Tracey had gone. She'd taken her own life. I was devastated. I was still only a kid myself and had no idea how to deal with the news.

I would have gone to see her if I'd known what she was planning. Of course I would as I loved her, but I hadn't made it and now she was gone. Could I have made a difference? The thought was still haunting me eight years on, but now I had an appreciation as to why she needed to escape.

She must have felt what I was feeling now. The future must have looked as bleak and uninviting for her as it now did for me.

I had no professional help from within or from outside of football while I struggled with my thoughts. I'd seen no doctors or medical experts on depression and I didn't feel able to tell anyone within my sport as there appeared little chance of finding any understanding.

I'd even pushed my loving wife away.

Now it was time to go. I was sure of that. I had the means and there was no-one to stop me. I put the phone down on mum and raced into the hotel. I had to do this before I could change my mind.

I lay on the bed and chucked one pill after another into my mouth, and after each batch of five or six tablets, I took a decent swig of whiskey.

I was relentless. I was dedicated to death. This was serious shit now. I couldn't stop myself and I didn't want to.

Inside five minutes 40 sleeping tablets and several anti-inflammatories were in my system along with half a bottle of whiskey.

I'd surely done it. I don't recall much, there was no memory of an inner-peace, no sense of relief, no life flashing before me, just a longing to fall asleep for one last time.

But then I thought of my dad. I needed to say thank you and goodbye to my big, powerful father who had always been there for me, supporting me during every step of the way in my life.

I had followed his path into professional sport and he was one of the major reasons why I had travelled as far as I had.

Even in my semi-conscious state, I told myself I had to speak to him one last time. I don't believe it was a sub-conscious cry for help or one last attempt to get people to see and understand my problems as for all I knew my dad could have been on the other side of the country, unable to make a difference.

I wasn't panicking. In fact, I was eerily calm. I told dad I'd done something stupid. I told him I'd taken loads of pills. He freaked out, while I crashed around the room before collapsing on the bed and passing out.

It turned out dad was close by.

I had been drifting in and out of consciousness for what seemed like hours when dad burst in with a couple of members of the hotel staff.

I was groggy, my eyes were heavy and shut, but I could still hear. My dad's voice was faint, but full of concern: 'Champ, wake up,' he was repeating over and over again.

Then my world went black and silent. I assumed this was death.

I was wrong. I came round the next morning in hospital. Sofia was there with my mum, dad, cousins, Tracey's mum Kim, my elder sister Rebecca, everyone I loved deeply, they were all there. And they were all in tears. They were expecting, hoping, to hear some words to suggest I'd reached rock bottom and that I'd now fight my way back up.

"It didn't work then," I said, finally realising I was still alive. My mum stormed out of the room, appalled at what I had just said.

And I wasn't joking. I was disappointed to still be around. The nurse said that one or two more pills would have done the job and that I was lucky, but that was the last thing I felt.

Dad had been 10 minutes away when I called him and he'd arrived in the nick of time. That was also lucky, but frustrating from my illogical point of view.

I instantly regretted not blagging some more pills from the Charlton medical staff.

I'd failed to kill myself and I was still depressed. More so because of what I'd just put those I loved the most through. My nightmare was to continue.

I was discharged that morning, so I got up, picked up my kit and went off to the football ground for treatment on my hamstring.

Life must go on even if you didn't want it to.

CHAPTER 2

'BREAKING DOWN, PHYSICALLY AND MENTALLY'

Depression was not a dirty word in the world of football in 2009 when I tried to kill myself, but it was pretty much an unspoken word.

The powers that be at Charlton must have known about my suicide bid. I'd been treated in Dartford Hospital and that was the hospital the club used as routine for their injured players.

They also used to put loads of footballers up at the Bexleyheath Marriott, new signings mostly, so word I expect would have got back to the club about what I'd tried to do.

But no-one at Charlton said anything and I didn't utter a word to anyone about the darkest night of my life. I didn't realise it at the time, but that was a massive mistake on my part.

Staying silent is the last thing I should have done. How on earth would that help fellow sufferers come out and admit they needed help?

And how on earth would that force people within the game to understand and then confront the problem?

The only time to my knowledge my illness was mentioned by a Charlton official was in a phone call to my agent from Phil Parkinson, the manager who had signed me and who had become increasingly, and understandably, frustrated that I had hardly set foot on the pitch for him and his club.

Parkinson mentioned to my agent that he was aware that I had 'issues'. That was it. No attempt to find out what was wrong with me or how to help me.

He'd in my opinion dismissed my problems with a term that covered everything yet meant nothing. Perhaps, the club didn't what to get involved, that's how it seemed to me anyway.

I know the world of professional football is a cut-throat business and players are often treated like commodities to be bought and sold on a whim, but at the end of the day we are human beings with feelings.

We cry, we get upset, we get scared. We have families who suffer alongside us.

But every time I bumped into Parkinson, he seemed to shy away from me and avoid eye-contact. He seemed embarrassed, not knowing what to say to me.

He was far from a bad bloke though. I accepted his frustration with a player he had signed being unable to play, but he just had no idea how to deal with someone with my condition – as far as I could tell no-one in football had that knowledge or awareness.

Talking about personal issues like depression is impossible for many men. Especially in football where we're all supposed to be big, tough and ruthless.

I don't have a problem with Parkinson at all. He gave me a chance when others were ignoring me after all and he never lost his temper with me despite my failure to get fit for him.

He just seemed uncomfortable with my situation and I couldn't blame him for that. It was the culture within football that was to blame.

I don't for one minute believe that I was the only one suffering from depression in the world of football.

I suspect some of the biggest stars in the game will be suffering from the illness now and they will be even more reluctant than I was to talk openly because they fear they have more to lose. They will believe the bigger the fame the bigger the shame, but that is no longer the case, even if it ever was.

Players at every level need someone to talk to. It has to be someone they can relate to, who knows and understands the pressures of professional sport, so they can speak with the benefit of experience.

The outsider, the fan, the man on the street looks at footballers and thinks that because they earn big money they should be happy. That just isn't true. We have the same strains and stresses as the average working man.

We have money problems, we get divorced and we get separated from our kids. Just because some of us earn thousands of pounds a week (or obviously much more at the very top of the game) doesn't mean we don't get hurt.

I'm sure if players knew there was an expert on hand, preferably one with experience of the professional game, they would be able to open up and avoid the situation I found myself in.

When I spoke about my experiences in the Daily Mail, I had calls from footballers who thanked me for putting my problems out in the open.

Darren Eadie, an old football mate was one, and a few others who I'd played with also got in touch. They were also suffering in a similar way and they were relieved that a fellow player had found the courage to speak in public about their personal problems.

It helped them avoid the excessive lengths I went to. They sought help and their lives improved as a result.

The death of Gary Speed had convinced me I needed to speak out. I wouldn't have been able to live with myself if another footballer had taken his own life while I stayed quiet.

I wish now that I had spoken out sooner.

No-one else should go through what I experienced. There is no need as help should now be available, unlike during my bad time. I was a Charlton player and yet they had lost interest in me, because I'd hardly managed to play for them, rather than because they were affected by my pretty blatant show of despair in that hotel room.

They would release me at the end of the season to complete pretty much the worst 12 months of my life. They were probably glad to get rid of me.

I'd actually gone there confident I could make a difference. Charlton were riding high at the top of League One and they had some decent players like Jonjo Shelvey, Christian Dailly and Deon Burton at the club.

I made my debut as a substitute in a 0-0 draw against Oldham and that was the third game in a row that Charlton had failed to score so I felt sure I would soon get in the side.

But I just couldn't stay fit. I'd feel niggles and pulls in training that would keep me out for a couple of weeks at a time and the next time I played, again as a substitute, we were knocked out of the FA Cup by non-league Northwich Victoria.

I ended up playing just 14 games for Charlton and I didn't start any of them. It was a shame because they were basically a good club full of lovely people, but I managed just a solitary goal, at Southampton in the Johnstone's Paint Trophy.

I know I could have helped them if I had stayed fit. I'd won two promotions in my career by that time so I had the experience of succeeding in tense situations, but my body was continually letting me down.

Charlton went on to lose in the League One play-off semi-finals but I didn't feel part of the squad by then.

Psychologically, I was also spent. I was scared and I was panicking. I was at the end of a personal road that started to veer off in difficult directions at my previous club, Coventry City.

It was there that I now believe my depression really started to set in. I'd battled through plenty in my life before then, but the injuries had started to pile up while I was at Coventry and it was the injuries that tipped me over the edge.

Plenty of other personal experiences before I arrived at Coventry probably didn't help either.

I'd seen my fantastic parents split up in acrimonious circumstances. I'd been uncomfortable at times living with either of them, which had helped propel me into a disastrous relationship and first marriage.

I'd been the victim of domestic violence and I'd been sexually abused by an adult woman as a 10-year-old boy who was lodger at my dad's pub.

I'd been through a messy divorce after having my name and parenting skills rubbished in the national press by my then wife.

I'd been temporarily forced away from my first two children by constant rows with their mother who had also tried to take me to the cleaners financially.

I'd found God as a born-again Christian early in my career, but then found that used against me in order to drive me from my hometown club, Crystal Palace.

All these things could have been triggers for my illness, but the thought of finishing in football brought me down mentally in an instant.

When I picked up the injury that effectively brought my Football League career to an end (I was playing for Coventry against Birmingham at the time), my attitude towards life in general just changed. The first thoughts of suicide started to drift into my head.

Even during the darkest days of my divorce, my lack of contact with my children and the loss of my Premier League status, I could still make other people happy just by scoring goals and playing well.

But even that wasn't going to happen anymore, not if this injury proved as bad as I feared.

There was no counselling available, or none that I was aware of. All I encountered was the ruthlessness of certain people in professional football.

I'd been taught how to hold the ball up and how to score goals, but there was nothing in the coaching manual covering how to deal with a sudden loss of form, fame and income.

There was also nothing in the coaching manuals to deal with serious personal issues like the loss of a relative to suicide.

I was displaying all the classic symptoms of depression. I was anxious, nervous, tired and irritable. I became detached emotionally from everyone I loved and I was afraid that this was how my life would be forever.

One of the drawbacks of depression is the self-inflicted loneliness. Your circle of friends becomes tiny and you feel remote from even your closest family members.

I was scared of being alone with my thoughts and yet I kept myself away from my friends and family. I couldn't relax and I certainly couldn't sleep as my head was just full of negativity.

I'd drag myself to work and go through a charade of well-being with my colleagues, but back at the hotel room I'd just surrender to the solitude and cry.

I'd enjoyed my time at Coventry when I first went there. They paid Norwich City £600,000 for me (rising to £1 million) and they offered me a decent escape route from the personal troubles I was having with my first wife.

Coventry actually played Norwich in the Championship two days after I signed. I wasn't allowed to play, but we won 3-0 and the Norwich fans started singing the song they had created for me when I scored twice on my debut for them against Ipswich a couple of years earlier, which was cool.

Coventry manager Mickey Adams was an old school boss who liked his players to run. He played me a few times on the left of midfield as he had Dele Adebola, Stern John and Kevin Kyle as strikers, the position I preferred to play and where I had made my name.

I did well out of position though. I felt sharp and although I only nicked the odd goal here and there, I was creating plenty of chances for the other players.

I remember terrorising Greg Halford in a TV game against Colchester. He was supposed to be the next top right-back, but I was nut-megging him for fun.

I didn't score but I set two goals up and we won 2-1.

I did score the occasional key goal most notably when we beat

Wolves 2-1 at the Ricoh Arena when they were fighting hard for promotion.

Jordan Henderson was playing on loan for us at the time and he set me up for a lovely dinked finish. The ball took ages to dribble over the line, but then the crowd erupted. I'd lived for moments like that for the previous 12 years and the excitement, the adrenaline rush, was just the same.

Henderson was a quality young midfielder and seemed destined for the top back then. I was happy to see him move to a big club like Liverpool, but I am amazed that he hasn't, so far at least, found his feet at that level.

Unfortunately, my own euphoria after the Wolves game didn't last. In my very next appearance, I was playing well against Birmingham at the Ricoh when my achilles snapped.

And there you have the amazing highs and the demoralising lows of professional football in the space of a fortnight. It's no wonder so many players struggle to stay on an even keel.

There never seems to be any periods of calm. You're either on top of the world or right down in the dumps. The newspapers don't help as headlines are either unrestrained joy or total misery.

I was devastated when I collapsed in that Birmingham match. It felt like someone had two-footed me from behind but in reality I'd collapsed with no-one around me. I was in agony for about 10 minutes and then my whole leg just went numb.

Mike, the physio, told me later that my achilles felt like scrambled egg. I was 31 at the time and if I'm honest I never really recovered from that one.

My mind certainly gave up on me. Was this the end? How do footballers cope with the sudden collapse of their career? I was pretty sure I would struggle as I'd paid little attention to my future beyond when the next goal would arrive.

The Birmingham match took place towards the end of February and that was my season over and there was a chance I wouldn't be ready to start the following campaign.

Chris Coleman was Coventry manager by then. I'd played with

him in my younger days at Crystal Palace.

He was, at least, sympathetic to my cause as he'd suffered a similar injury himself. My contract, which was slightly better than the one I'd left behind at Norwich, was up at the end of the season, but chairman Ray Ranson offered me a one-year deal worth a quarter of what I was on, and only on a month by month basis until my injuries had cleared up.

That offer immediately put me under pressure as I don't care who you are or what profession you are in. If your wages drop by over two thirds that causes you problems, especially if you were already regularly dipping into a £15,000 overdraft like I was.

We all have a certain lifestyle to which we become used to. Mine was being wrecked, but I had no choice to accept. I had kids to feed after all.

Sure, we earned good money, but our professional lifespan was short. I'd earned well at Norwich, but a costly divorce had set me back to square one financially.

Everything I'd ever strived for in my professional life was about to come to a shuddering halt.

I'd been doing something for over a decade that I'd loved doing, scoring goals and enjoying the worship from fans that comes with the territory. My world was about to come crashing down in spectacular style.

~ BETTER DAYS ~

It was a shame as I'd seen some good days at Coventry.

Iain Dowie had taken over as Coventry manager when Adams left. He was a good bloke and I got on well with him.

He was a much better coach than player. In fact he used to say he was a crap player who made the most of the ability he had, something he insisted we all did.

Iain was an enthusiast. He loved the game and he made it a mission to get the best out of every single one of his players.

He was so passionate himself it couldn't help but rub off on the players, but some of them found him a bit overbearing and didn't respond to his methods.

Iain liked to spend time individually with the players and I enjoyed that. The sessions he put on for the strikers were all good as far as I was concerned.

Iain had a great start to his managerial career at Palace and, although he hasn't been as successful since, he always had a right go and I respected that.

I'd finished the previous season on the sidelines as well, but in the summer we went to Tenerife for pre-season training and I was flying.

I was winning all the running races in my group by miles. Dowie was impressed and he told the other players that the reason I was starting the first game of the next season was because my attitude towards pre-season training had been better than anyone else's.

I duly played against Barnsley in the opening game and I scored in a 4-1 away win.

I scored in the next game against Hull as well and I felt brilliant. I played most of the first eight matches but then, after I'd played well in a 1-1 draw at Palace, I did my knee in training.

Injuries had started to creep back into my game, silly little things like pulled muscles and irritating niggles. When I played, I did well; but I wasn't out there as often as I or the club would have liked.

This knee injury required an operation though and kept me out for two months.

When I returned, Coleman had replaced Dowie as manager and he had Steve Kean with him as coach.

It was a weird situation having a man as my manager who I'd played with and who I'd been out clubbing with. In all honesty I never felt comfortable with it.

There was one bizarre incident with Coleman which started when I had to pull out of a reserve team game because I had some personal stuff involving my kids to deal with.

I phoned him up and explained what had happened, but the

longer the conversation went on the more bizarrely Coleman was behaving. He was talking so weirdly it did cross my mind he might have had a long lunch so I was struggling to take him seriously.

He certainly wasn't himself and all of a sudden he started to get aggressive with me.

Now that wasn't like him and then out of the blue he challenged me to a fight in the boxing ring which I found really funny.

"Dukey," he said. "Let's get the gloves on as I want to smash your face in." I couldn't believe what I was hearing as it was so silly it was funny, but I agreed and said I'd get my dad, a former British boxing champion who still ran a gym, to fix it up.

I told the rest of the players and Kean, and the lads were buzzing. They reckoned they could sell tickets and make a fortune.

The thought of their manager getting beaten up also appealed to some.

The next day, I told Kean the fight was set, but when Coleman turned up he was so embarrassed and clearly regretted his bravado. He hugged me and told me he'd be stupid to fight me so we laughed it off.

The lads were disappointed though.

I generally got on well with Kean, apart from one occasion when I trained poorly.

My concentration was never the best when I was doing drills. Kean had put on a simple crossing drill, but I hadn't done it before and I was struggling.

Kean laid into me in front of everyone. He was yelling and screaming, basically making me feel useless, so I had it out with him afterwards demanding to know if he had a problem with me. Kean was shocked by my reaction, but he respected the fact that I confronted him face to face and we never had a problem after that.

He was basically a very good coach, but I never saw him as a potential manager.

I grew to like Steve though. He was very honest and if he made a mistake he would hold his hands up, unlike some managers and coaches who blame everyone but themselves.

He did me a massive favour when Charlton were thinking about signing me. They asked him about me and Steve said that if they kept me fit they would have one hell of a player on their books and that was really good of him.

Steve had a terrible time at Blackburn, but not because he's a bad manager. Football is being run more and more by business people and they can't stop themselves getting involved more than they should.

Things then get too complicated behind the scenes and the manager becomes an easy target, but Steve is a strong personality and he will come through the other side okay.

We still speak now and again today and the way he dealt with all the aggro at Blackburn is a great credit to him.

Leon Best moved to Coventry from Southampton while I was there. He was a great lad and I have enjoyed seeing him scoring goals in the Premier League for Newcastle.

He was a kid when he came to the Ricoh and he looked up to me. We were mates. I once showed him a picture of the wedding venue for my second marriage, Gosfield Hall in Braintree.

It was a stunning place. It was just a massive, gorgeous building with acres and acres of beautiful gardens.

He looked at me, looked at the pics and then looked back admiringly at me. 'Oh my God,' he said.

'Is that your house? Wow that's amazing.'

 I laughed out loud, but let him sit on what he'd said for a while before telling him the truth.

'You had me going,' he admitted. 'But I believed you because you're Leon McKenzie and you've scored goals in the Premier League. To me it's possible you could have earned enough to live in a house like this!"

It was actually quite humbling to hear this from a young player. Not enough youngsters in the game these days show that sort of respect to a senior player.

I love 'Besty' to bits. I have a lot of time for him and I hope he goes on to have a great career.

~ 100 GOALS ~

Sadly, I couldn't shake my injuries off. I ruptured a thigh muscle against Southampton and tried to carry on thinking it was just a dead leg, but I succeeded only in ripping the muscle off the tendon.

I was out for three months, coming back to score my 100th professional goal against Norwich in my first game back, on the opening day of the 2008-09 season.

Clinton Morrison set me up for a tap-in, but I celebrated like I'd won the World Cup for England. I'd come on as a sub and some Norwich fans thought I'd gone over the top with my celebrations after the goal clinched a 2-0 win.

But it was just relief. I'd been sitting on 99 goals for six months (including the closed season) and wasn't sure I'd ever get to 100. I made a point of going over to the Norwich fans after the game and applauding them so I hope they forgive me.

I soldiered on at Coventry at the start of the following season when Charlton came calling with an offer of £3,500 week for a season.

I don't know why Coventry couldn't have done that for me. They could easily have secured my future for another season on a living wage.

I felt that they'd fucked with my mind which had already been coming under severe strain because of my run of injuries.

Coventry were happy to let me go though and so off I went to Charlton.

I would be back in London which was a bonus. I would be away from family though which would turn out to be a disaster for me.

CHAPTER 3

'THE KEYS TO NORWICH'

Adam Drury patted me on the back and said: "Leon, do you realise what you've just done? You've just earned the keys to the city of Norwich."

If the last days at Charlton were the worst of my career, the best had arrived at Norwich City. Things started perfectly for me at the club and I rode a wave of momentum for a good two years before off-the-field issues caused my departure.

I moved to Norwich from Peterborough. At Peterborough I'd been training at a local technical college, but when I drove to Norwich with my agent Tim Webb to meet manager Nigel Worthington and his assistant Doug Livermore to discuss personal terms we met at the club's Colney training ground.

I'd been used to seeing dog mess on the training pitches at Peterborough, so when I drove through the gates at Colney I was pretty much sure I was going to sign there and then. This was a spectacular venue compared to what I'd been used to.

This was a different planet. I was about to swap Aldi for Waitrose in football terms and as long as I felt wanted, I'd be a Norwich player by the end of that day.

Livermore did most of the talking in his high-pitched Scouse accent. The plans Norwich had to secure promotion to the Premier

League and to stay there seemed sound and they believed I could play a big part in helping them achieve their goals.

I was never into football for the money so when I was offered £3,600 a week – about twice what I was getting at Peterborough – I accepted it without haggling. The most important thing for me was the positive vibe I picked up from Worthington and I knew from that first meeting that we would have a strong relationship. I'd gone up a division in standard to Division One with the chance of going even higher to the promised land of the Premier League. Norwich were going well when I signed in December 2003. They were in the thick of the promotion race and were due to play Ipswich in a massive derby match at Portman Road the Sunday after I arrived, but I didn't expect to play.

True, I had been banging in the goals in training and it was obvious the other Norwich lads were watching me closely and could see that I had a bit about me.

But it would be a gamble for Worthington to throw me straight into the side, especially as he'd just signed another striker in Matt Svensson. Playing two newcomers alongside each other (although I had played briefly with Matt at Palace) would be a risk in such an important game and Worthington wasn't a manager known to take risks.

I was happy to see Matt there though, as he was a clever player who I was sure would help me make my mark at this level.

Darren Huckerby had finished a loan spell at Norwich just before me and Matt arrived at Carrow Road so when Worthington called me and Svensson into his office after training one morning we didn't really know what to expect.

One of us probably had a chance of playing as 'Hucks' had left.

After a few questions about how we were settling in, Worthington dropped a bombshell about us both starting at Ipswich. 'Were we up for it?' he asked.

The smile on my face told Worthington all he needed to know and he told me there and then that my debut would be in the biggest game of the club's season.

At the time, I wasn't really aware just how big a deal this game was, but I knew it was a match to be shown live on television so I was buzzing when I left the manager's office. The build-up in the local press then helped me realise that this was a game both sides wanted to win more than any other.

I said when I first arrived at Carrow Road that I wanted to set my marker down quickly and this was obviously the perfect game in which to do it.

The Norwich team that day was: *Robert Green, Mark Edworthy, Adam Drury, Malky Mackay, Curtis Fleming, Phil Mulryne, Paul McVeigh, Gary Holt, Ian Henderson, Leon McKenzie, Matt Svensson. Subs: Iwan Roberts, Jim Brennan, Paul Crichton, Damien Francis, Ryan Jarvis.*

This was my opportunity, another chance to show everyone who I was and what I was about. I was playing with and against some seriously good players now.

George Santos was the Ipswich player detailed to mark me. He was a big lump, but I wasn't afraid of him and I terrorised him and the other Ipswich defenders all game. Santos went off at half-time and by then I'd claimed a debut goal.

After 37 minutes, Paul McVeigh, a classy player who I loved playing with, whipped a ball into the penalty area and it fell for me about eight yards from goal.

I struck it left-footed and the net was soon rippling, and I was soon being swamped by everyone on the Norwich bench as I'd run there to celebrate.

At this point, I was really performing and 15 minutes from the end Gary Holt, a player better known for his athleticism than his passing ability, sped off down the wing.

I instinctively pulled off my marker and waited for the cross to come in. I waited and waited and felt Gary was going to waste the opportunity, but finally the ball was on its way and I turned again, spun, and soared above a defender before heading home.

Defenders often used to under-estimate my heading ability. I scored many goals with my head as a result.

None more important than this one though and this time I ran to the Norwich fans to celebrate. My arms were out like an aeroplane and I then pointed to the name on the back of my shirt.

"This is who I am," I was screaming. "I am here to stay." I felt like a million dollars and what Drury, who I'd played with at Peterborough, said to me after the game was true.

This match didn't just mean the world to the players, the management and the fans. The whole of Norwich, and indeed Norfolk, demanded we won games against Ipswich, so to be the match-winner on my debut for the club was an incredible thrill. The fact that we'd gone top of the league as a result seemed incidental!

Mind you, I didn't celebrate with the lads afterwards thanks to the drugs testers.

I was selected to give a urine sample straight after the match, but I'd put so much into the 90 minutes I was totally dehydrated. I just couldn't pee.

Two hours I waited. There was just me, a test tube and a tester in a room. By the time I got out, the stadium was deserted.

The TV station and the rest of the media had naturally wanted to interview me, but I couldn't do that. Peterborough manager Barry Fry, my old boss, was the TV studio guest and he said that I'd played so well I probably had been on something! (This was a joke of course.)

Being dragged away from the post-match celebrations did take the edge off, but the papers were a good read the next day.

And as a result of just one game in Norwich colours, a terrace song was created just for me. I never tire of hearing: 'Oh McKenzie, he scored against the scum, oh McKenzie he scored another one.'

I can walk back through Norwich now and people will still recognise me and congratulate me. I remember having a stroll through the city centre with my kids a few years after I'd left the club and hearing some geezer start singing my song while leaning out of his office window.

After my debut, I felt like I now had the opportunity to crack the big time again (I'd played briefly in the Premier League as a teenager with Crystal Palace) and I wasn't going to let it pass.

I'd seen players get their dream move and shrivel up mentally and get nowhere. That wasn't going to be me.

I'd always worked hard and scored my goals at Peterborough, but I was playing with class players now so I'd be a fool to mess this opportunity up.

We won the first three games after my move. I scored my next goal in the third game at Derby, a penalty in a 4-0 win which strangely prompted one Norwich player to fall out with me.

Not that I knew it at the time.

Welsh international striker Iwan Roberts was at Norwich when I joined. He had been a good player in his day and he was more of a household name than me, but he was at the back-end of his career when I turned up.

He must have resented my presence at the club because he wrote about me in his own book which was published while we were both still at Norwich.

He ran me down all because of an incident against Derby which made me feel very uncomfortable.

I was fouled in the penalty area and I insisted I took the penalty, and I scored.

Roberts was the club's penalty-taker in those days, but he didn't say anything at the time. He made up for it in his book.

Apparently, he was desperately trying to get to 100 goals for Norwich and he was on 94. A penalty was obviously an easy chance to move closer to that milestone, but I had denied him the opportunity.

He called me, shallow, in his book which disheartened me. People often mistook my confidence for arrogance and Iwan had clearly misread my character.

The truth is I wanted to take that penalty because I knew I would score and Norwich had spent all that money on me to get the goals that would get them into the Premier League. It was my job to score goals for them and I didn't care how they arrived.

And to be fair, I didn't even know about Iwan and his 100 goal target.

If I had known, and bearing in mind we were 3-0 up at the time, I would definitely have let him have the ball. I liked Iwan and I knew he was a bit of a folk hero at the club as well as a seriously good player, so there's no way I would have gone out of my way to upset him.

I didn't like what I read in his book though, so I confronted Iwan the next time I saw him. I'm a sensitive person really, but if someone comes for me and I don't deserve it, I will go back at them.

Iwan was shocked at how angry I was. He mumbled something about 'trying to sell a book' (something I can fully appreciate now!) But he knew he'd made a mistake and the incident itself was just a misunderstanding.

We've made up properly since as well. There's no bitterness between me and Iwan and we still speak to each other now and again.

'Hucks' had returned to the club by then which obviously gave everyone on and off the field a fantastic boost and we went on to win six of our last seven matches to clinch promotion to the Premier League.

We banged in loads of goals. 'Hucks' made a massive difference and we scored five at Burnley and five at home to Walsall.

I scored four goals in five games towards the end of the season so I did my bit. I wasn't always in the starting line-up, but I scored nine goals in total which made it 20 for the season as I'd scored 11 for Peterborough before I left.

Norwich actually won the league by eight points (with a record total of 94 points) ahead of West Brom to end a 10-year absence from the top flight. It was a double celebration for me as my old club Crystal Palace went on to win promotion as well through the play-offs after a fantastic end to the season under Iain Dowie.

The first six months of my career at Norwich were just fantastic. My marriage was under pressure for all sorts of reasons, but my football life was just perfect.

~ HITTING THE BIG TIME ~

The Premier League was the place to be. It's where I felt I belonged at that time.

I was playing well and I was at a great club. We were desperate to succeed. I was confident I'd do well, but there was a nagging doubt about the club's prospects as we didn't sign too many players, apart from a young winger called David Bentley on loan from Arsenal.

Darren Huckerby was there though and Dean Ashton came later. They were the two best players I played with in my entire career. 'Hucks' was a real crowd favourite and the rest of the squad loved him as well. He was a great player.

He would just glide past defenders and he would instinctively know where I was in the penalty area. 'Hucks' was the main source of Norwich goals whether he was scoring them or creating them.

'Deano' joined us from Crewe. He had a big price tag and a big reputation, but when the lads watched him train we were all looking at each other thinking 'oh my god, how much did he cost? What a complete waste of money'.

He was the worst trainer I ever saw. He looked off the pace, he didn't compete and he was just so sluggish, we all thought the manager had dropped an almighty clanger.

But we were all aware of the number of goals he had scored at Crewe so we weren't ready to write him off that quickly.

And we were right not to, as on the pitch 'Deano' was simply brilliant, the complete opposite of how he was in training.

He was an old school centre-forward, good in the air, strong, he held the ball up well and he had incredible vision. He could finish as well.

He always did the business on match day and he was so easy to play with. I just used to run in behind defenders knowing the ball would land just where I wanted it.

It was no surprise when he was getting linked with even bigger clubs than ours. It was no surprise when he started getting tipped for an England call-up.

He had to retire early because of injury while he was a West Ham player and that was such a shame, especially as he was only 26.

I know Dean struggled to come to terms with his retirement, but he has a young family now and he is content. I'm not sure I would have coped so well if I'd had to pack football in that early.

If he had stayed, fit Dean was a certainty to join one of the biggest clubs and become an England regular, that's how highly we all rated him at Norwich.

Dean also enjoyed playing with me. He was kind enough to pen some words when he heard about this book.

He said: "When I first joined Norwich, I wasn't sure how I was going to be received by the other strikers in the team as generally being in competition for 'top' striker can leave a frosty atmosphere.

"Leon more than any other striker I've played with made me feel so comfortable and I never felt he was out to make life awkward. He is outwardly very confident and that certainly rubbed off on me and he made me feel like I was a top player.

Without a shadow of a doubt, if Leon hadn't been my strike partner when I first went to Norwich, I wouldn't have done as well as I did at the club.

He is a top player and a lot of the work he did off the ball to help me out went unnoticed. He knew where the goal was and when he did score... well what a show off!

I had no idea of any troubles away from football and in his head. He must have hidden it well as every day he seemed in a good, jokey mood which is why he was so popular in the dressing room. He has been brilliant with me at and away from football and I will always be grateful for how he helped me in my career."

I loved those days in the Premier League. I had become a much better player in the last six months because of my Norwich team-mates and now I was competing strongly against some outstanding players.

I wasn't always in the starting line-up at the start of the Premier League season, but I was coming off the bench and doing okay. I just had to wait for my chance.

I played the last few minutes as we drew our first game at home to Palace, but our second game was at Old Trafford and that was the day that I realised I could compete at this level.

I came on as a substitute again and I didn't score even though I should have as I had one chance on my left foot, but I screwed my shot just wide of Tim Howard's post from about 12 yards.

No, my big moment arrived when I dumped Roy Keane on his backside and that was a big boost to my confidence.

Keane was playing at the back for United that day so I was right up against him from the start.

We were soon chasing for a loose ball and I thought: 'I don't care who you are, I'm having that ball off you'. I shoulder barged him and he went flying. There was a gasp from the Old Trafford crowd as no-one did that to Keane, but it made me feel 10 feet tall.

Like all pros, I respected Keane as a great player, one of the best, but I was desperate to make my own name and even the top players weren't going to get in my way.

We lost that game 2-1 after Alan Smith scored a sensational goal with a superb, technically-perfect volley, but the Premier League was my stage now and I wanted to shine.

There were close to 70,000 people watching that game which was simply incredible for everyone at Norwich City. We had decent crowds and a brilliantly loyal support, but 70,000 spectators was a different ball game.

Unfortunately, the team didn't win for ages (it was the 14th game of the season before Norwich beat Southampton 2-1 at Carrow Road) even though we came close at times.

We never lost heart though and the fans stayed with the players and the management. They could see we were giving everything and we were slowly improving.

We fought back from 2-0 down to draw 2-2 at Newcastle when Gary Doherty scored the equaliser just three minutes after I came on as a substitute.

We played well at Spurs and at home to Aston Villa, but drew both games 0-0. I came on as a substitute in both matches, but I was getting itchy feet as we weren't scoring many goals and yet I wasn't playing many minutes.

Worthington often played one up front and that was always going to be 'Hucks', but eventually I started a game against Portsmouth which we drew 2-2 and I kept my place for the next few matches. And then I scored my first Premier League goal, against Everton at Carrow Road, past my old Palace team-mate Nigel Martyn.

I was playing up against David Weir and I couldn't believe how slow he was. I was all over him, I was far too quick, far too sharp and far too clever.

Anyway, we were soon chasing a long ball and I held Weir off, raced away from him and slotted the ball through Nigel's legs. I didn't look at Nigel as he was a Palace legend and I didn't want him to be embarrassed!

We were 2-0 down in that game, got back to 2-2, but ended up losing 3-2 in another of the great games we had that season. Unfortunately, we didn't win enough of them.

It took an amazing effort in the second-half of the season for us to even have a chance of avoiding an immediate relegation.

We drew too many games for a start. We picked up a good point at Manchester City and the following week we drew 1-1 with Blackburn, but we let them equalise late on after they'd played with 10 men for half the game.

I also remember we were 4-1 down against Middlesbrough and drew 4-4 after scoring three goals in the last 10 minutes. I came on as a sub and scored the third goal before Adam Drury claimed the equaliser, but there were too many games where we came so close to winning and just couldn't get over the line.

~ BEATING UNITED ~

We only won seven Premier League games all season, but it was almost enough to stay up. The most memorable was a win against Manchester United which arrived when we really needed it towards the end of the season.

United were chasing Chelsea, unsuccessfully as it turned out, for the title. They clearly felt we provided easy pickings as they left Wayne Rooney and Cristiano Ronaldo on the bench.

Before a game, I'd prepare mentally for what I hoped would happen. I'd go off to a quiet place and visualise scoring and celebrating. I really fancied I would score that day as I was on form.

I'd actually been on a decent little scoring run. I'd scored against Manchester City and Chelsea and even though we'd lost both matches I felt I was making an excellent contribution.

I was certainly hyped up for this one as were all our players to be fair. I remember that in the tunnel before the game I had a little look across to Rio Ferdinand, and I was saying in my head: 'I'm going to give you some today.'

I just wanted to get out onto the pitch and compete with players like that. Some players would freeze, but I came from a proud boxing family and as my dad and my world champion uncle used to box better in the bigger fights, I also played my best in the biggest of occasions.

The game was on television and we played well. I was doing my bit even though Ferdinand, the best defender I ever faced, was on top of his game.

And the chance to make my mark arrived when Youssef Safri tackled Rooney and passed it out wide to 'Hucks'. 'Huck's slipped it quickly to Dean Ashton and I just sensed this was my moment. Dean's cross, as usual, was perfect. I steadied myself, focussed totally on the ball and when it reached me on my left foot I knew I would score.

And as soon as my volley slammed into the net I was off and running. I took my shirt off to celebrate this one (I was boxing fit back then!) put out my hands and accepted the acclaim from the Norwich fans behind the goal.

'Deano' had opened the scoring about 10 minutes earlier and we eventually beat them 2-0. Even Rooney and Ronaldo couldn't come on and save them.

It was my day that day and I'd say it was the greatest moment of my career. As a team, we felt that if we could beat one of the best teams in the country we should really be good enough to stay up. Unfortunately we only drew 3-3 at Palace in our next game after being 3-1 up, but then we did beat Newcastle and Charlton with late goals so we thought things were finally going our way.

Incidentally, I scored in the game at Selhurst Park and upset a few Palace fans with my goal celebration as I ran down the touchline with my finger over my lips, but that was directed at a former manager Alan Smith and current chairman Simon Jordan, the two men who forced me out of my hometown club.

I was telling them that I was doing my talking on the pitch, unlike them.

~ NIGHTMARE AT THE COTTAGE ~

After the morale-boosting win over United, we kept fighting to give ourselves a chance. We lost a crazy game 4-3 at Southampton. I equalised to make it 3-3 at half-time, but they went on to score a late winner.

We then recovered to beat Birmingham 1-0 in our final home match of the season to keep us alive going into the final game of the season at Fulham.

It was an exciting final day as four different clubs could have gone down and we fancied our chances of survival. Fulham had nothing to play for and we were confident if we got at them early they wouldn't want to know.

I started up front with Dean Ashton at Craven Cottage and we knew we could cause Fulham's defenders problems with our movement and strength.

Leon McKenzie

Instead we went 1-0 down to an early goal from Brian McBride and went on lose 6-0. It was a complete capitulation, a total embarrassment and I really felt for our fans who had stuck with us through a really difficult season.

To this day, I don't know whether it was nerves or pressure or a combination of both, but we were all pathetic.

Our better players including me just didn't turn up. We were crushed. It was humiliating and I broke down in tears after the game as I felt I was never going to play in the top flight again, and sadly I was right.

I'd worked so hard to get back there and performed pretty well personally, but my dream had died. I was devastated for the fans, the manager, the staff and the board as they didn't deserve to see relegation confirmed by such an awful performance.

That game was a nightmare from start to finish, but we'd thrown away so many winning positions during the season which were just as costly.

I did win a player-of-the-season award, but that was scant consolation for relegation.

~ PREMIER MEMORIES ~

I did at least take some decent memories away from playing against big clubs and great players.

I came on as a substitute against Chelsea at Stamford Bridge early in the season after Matt Svensson picked up an early injury. They had John Terry, William Gallas and Wayne Bridge at the back.

One early run saw me leave Bridge on his backside. Terry was much harder to shake off and he was marking me at corners.

He would eye-ball me as some sort of challenge. I wasn't put off and told him to stay close or he'd be in trouble for letting me score.

Terry just used to smirk in a 'whatever' sort of way. He'd heard it all before I guess and usually come out on top.

Chelsea battered us at our place. They were a great team. They had Jose Mourinho in charge and they hadn't let in a goal for 9 games.

Joe Cole scored for them, but we didn't fold and when 'Hucks' sent in a set-piece I knew this was my chance.

I rose well above Terry and 'bang' my header flew past Petr Cech and into the net. What a moment and I immediately glanced back to see Terry's reaction, but he wasn't looking at me.

Mourinho mentioned me in his book as the player who ended their record run of clean sheets which was a proud moment for this South London boy.

Mind you, we still lost 3-1 and it had been 4-0 at their place!

Terry was a good player, but not a great player for me. For me Ferdinand was better. Before I faced him I knew he was quick and comfortable on the ball, but I hadn't realised how strong he was. He was the complete player, one of the greats.

Norwich was just a fantastic club. I had the best times of my career there, times that matched my debut for Palace at the age of 17.

So relegation was just a disaster for all of us. It should never have happened. We'd played well enough in the second half of the season to stay up.

I'd love to go back there one day and thank the fans and the club for giving me the chance to play at that level and to thank Delia Smith, my favourite chairman along with Ron Noades at Palace.

Delia pulled me to one side at the end-of-season awards. It was common knowledge at the club that I was going through a tough divorce from my first wife Vanessa and news had obviously reached the very top.

But Delia said that if there was anything she could help me with she would. She offered to send a chauffeur to pick the kids up from school if ever I couldn't make it and she gave me her number with an invitation to call if I ever needed her.

Her concern was very touching and it was a shame we took her club back down to Division One.

She, of course, achieved some notoriety with a half-time outburst during a match against Manchester City at Carrow Road.

Dean Ashton and I had given us a 2-0 lead, but City were level by half-time and Delia wasn't best pleased.

She took the mic on the pitch and delivered a 'let's be 'avin you' speech to try and get the crowd going.

The players didn't have a clue until afterwards what she had done, but she'd have been better off coming to the dressing room to speak as we went on to lose 3-2 to a last-minute Robbie Fowler goal!

Delia took some stick over her outburst and some of the players did think it was funny, but she is Norwich City through and through and the players generally loved her.

~ WORTHY MANAGER ~

I certainly wouldn't blame Worthington for our relegation. He had an old-fashioned way about him. He looked more like a school teacher than a football manager and when he lost his temper it was more likely to make the lads laugh than be afraid.

Once he got so mad with us he booted a skip and broke a bone in his foot, but the lads played for him because they liked and respected him.

He would bang on continually about work ethic. The only times he ever got angry were if he thought we hadn't put everything into a game or a training session.

It used to wind me up when he questioned my attitude because that's something I'd never been accused of before.

But I believe he had worked out how far he could push me and he was right. Moaning at me just made me more determined to prove him wrong by scoring a goal and the smile on his face whenever that happened told me I was right.

Worthington was pretty good at the man management side of things. He pulled me and Dean Ashton in training once just to tell us that he thought we were one of the most dangerous strike partnerships in the Premier League and we both left that day prepared to run through brick walls for him.

Worthington's biggest mistake was the fact that, in my opinion, the signings he made after our promotion weren't great, particularly Thomas Helveg who I felt was poor considering his reputation and experience.

Thomas came to us from Inter Milan having previously played for AC Milan, but he wasn't good for us.

It's a massive step up from Division One to the Premier League and, although it's honourable to be loyal to a successful squad, you also have to be realistic and try and get some players with top-flight experience (although judging by Helveg not from Serie A) through the door.

We let in almost 80 goals that season which was the highest in the division and that statistic just showed where most of our problems existed.

But it was the players who messed up that final game at Fulham not the manager. The squad Worthington trusted was still good enough to stay up, but we failed him and the fans.

I stayed with Norwich the following season (there were rumours of Charlton bidding £1.5 million for me which would have kept me in the Premier League, but nothing came of it), but the club had a massive hangover. We started the season as promotion favourites as players like Ashton, Huckerby and Robert Green were still at the club, but we started the season terribly.

We didn't win any of our first six league matches (although I did score the only goal in a Carling Cup win at MK Dons) and by the time we did start winning Division One matches I'd broken my ankle and had to sit out for three months.

I came back about Christmas time and in the second half of the season I played some games up front with Robert Earnshaw and we did well together.

We did threaten a promotion run at one point, but we lost our way in January and left ourselves too much to do. We eventually finished ninth which was not good enough.

The fans turned on Worthington during that season, but he stuck it out. I hated hearing the stick he got because he was a good man and a good manager.

I ended up with five goals that season, but I only played 20-odd matches.

I was becoming restless at the club now. I was having issues with my estranged wife that didn't help. I was then on the bench at the start of the 2006-07 season, but I handed in my transfer request because of off-the-field circumstances.

The manager was hurt and he said it felt like I'd kicked him in the teeth, but I had to get away from that area, not the football club.

I joined Coventry, but after a couple of months I called Worthington and thanked him for giving me a second chance in the Premier League and he said it was a pleasure, that I'd earned it, and thanked me back for doing so well for him.

He even wrote good things about me when I announced my retirement, saying : "Leon epitomised what Norwich was all about.

He was full of energy and he was a character in the dressing room who got on with everybody. He was a player that I really liked.

The biggest compliment I can pay him is to mention the 2-0 win over Manchester United when Leon scored a fantastic goal.

He deserved that and everyone in that team will go down in Norwich history for producing one of the best performances and the best results the club ever achieved.

I knew that he had difficult times off the field, but to his great credit, he did his work as a professional and whenever he needed help, I tried to be there for him."

~ VICIOUS RUMOURS ~

My decision to leave Norwich certainly had nothing to do with certain rumours circulating around the city at the time.

I've been the victim of some vicious speculation during my career. I admit I've done some bad stuff, some crazy stuff, but there are a couple of lies I just have to nail.

I was mates with Damien Francis at Norwich, good mates. We used to go at it in training, but never with any malice.

But during one training session me and Damien challenged for a high ball and I caught him in the face with my elbow.

It was an accident, but he was in a bad way. His cheekbone was smashed and the incident hit the papers.

But it also hit the internet along with the rumour that I'd harmed Damien on purpose for having an affair with my wife, Vanessa.

It was utter bullshit, total lies. I imagine it was people spending all day on internet sites, because they are bored, making stuff up about better people.

Trust me, no-one would have the balls to mess around with my wife. They would be in serious trouble, but the incident on the training ground was an accident and me and Damien are still friends today.

After the training ground incident, Damien came to my stag do and to my wedding to Sofia. I went to his wedding and that wouldn't have happened if he'd messed around with my first wife behind my back. He'd have been six feet under for a start, as I always remind him when I see him!

Damien lives abroad now, but when I speak to him we always remember the internet dickheads and have a good laugh about it.

Also, according to the trolls on the internet I spent some time in a mental home while I was at Norwich.

This one started because I was off training for a few days so some people started looking for possible reasons and stating them as fact.

The truth was my new girlfriend Sofia had just lost her father so she went to Spain for a few days to be with her family.

I wanted to be with her at this time. I was injured anyway so I contacted Worthington through the club physio, a great bloke called Neil Reynolds, and I was given permission to go.

It was a top gesture by the club, but while I was away supporting my girlfriend whose father had just passed away, other people were convinced I was having psychiatric treatment in a Norwich hospital.

Apparently some people still believe this stuff, but it's just rubbish. It was a private, personal trip I went on so I never explained publicly why I was absent, but that wasn't an excuse for small-minded people to peddle lies about me.

I only ever let my fists go once at Norwich and it left Youssef Safri needing stitches.

Safri was a very good footballer, but he loved a strong challenge, even in training and the lads would lose it with him on a regular basis.

There was a bit of larking about going on, in the treatment room one morning, but Safri wasn't in the mood and when I jumped on him in a jokey way while he was lying on one of the physio beds, he got angry. I'd only been mucking about, but he didn't see it that way and he shoved me away.

I went to give him a hug, but he shoved me again. I always give my 'opponent' one chance to reconsider his approach, but not two, so things turned a little ugly.

Neil, the physio, finally jumped in and ordered us both to the manager's office like naughty schoolkids, although kids were caned rather than fined £2,500 like we were.

Mind you, Worthington immediately rescinded my fine because he felt Safri was in the wrong. Me and Safri did make up and I pretty much got on with everyone at the club.

It was a real family club. Val the secretary, Terry the kitman and Dave the fitness coach, as well as the captain Craig Fleming were top, top people who just loved Norwich City.

I wasn't sure about Dave's declaration one day though that me and Huckerby had the most body fat. Everyone knew that had to be Lee Croft!!

CHAPTER 4

'WARRANT FOR MY ARREST'

Bizarrely, Charlton's reluctance to take more than a passing interest in my situation toughened me up. I found some resolve from somewhere, some determination to fight this depression.

I realised it was an illness. I realised I wasn't at all well, but I no longer felt it would claim me. I made progress, slow but definite progress.

I was cool with Charlton's decision to release me at the end of my one season there. Football's a business, more so nowadays, and there was no way they could justify keeping me on as I'd hardly played for them.

I'd opened up to Sofia. I was talking regularly to my parents and they were all doing what they could to lift my spirits.

I had bad days and I had good days (and that's still the case today). I was still far from my best mentally, but I wanted to live again and that was a start.

The day after my suicide bid, I discharged myself, had some treatment on my hamstring at Charlton before heading back to Northampton and the family home. I was back at Charlton the following day for more treatment and then returned to the Bexleyheath Marriott the following night.

On the surface that seemed risky, but I now had a support group. I was surrounded by the people who loved me and there is no doubt they saved my life by making me realise I had plenty of reasons to keep going.

I still had plenty of bad thoughts, but I wasn't alone anymore. My dad, my mum, my uncle Duke and Sofia, one of them would be with me all the time.

Sofia made sure my children were in constant contact as well. I look back now and realise how fortunate I was.

The hotel obviously held only horrible memories for me, but luckily I owned a flat nearby, which I had been renting out. That became vacant again so I moved in there which was another positive step for me. Every little step forward I made was a little victory in my head.

Believe me, making myself a cup of tea meant progress. When on my own, I never even bothered putting food in the microwave, I'd just go out and get takeaways, but the key for me now was keeping my head full of positive thoughts and that meant images of my family and the pain I would cause them by regressing.

I thought about my suicide bid every day for weeks. I would go over it again and again in my head, but I could sense a gradual return to normality.

Depression is triggered differently in different people. It might be money problems, it might be marital problems, or, as in my case, it might just be years of physical pain finally taking its toll and a fear of what the future held.

I now realised what my triggers were and I could fight them off whenever they threatened to attack me.

Visiting professionals in the medical world was recommended to me, but I never wanted to go down that route. I felt I could beat it myself as long as I kept Sofia, my parents and my children nearby.

I was having the odd bad day, but I was coping. I took no medication, I was relying on will power and I was proud of how I started to cope.

But then my world came crashing down around me again in circumstances that were just too ridiculous for words....

Towards the end of my year with Charlton I was on my way to hospital in Wimbledon for yet another injection in my knee when an unmarked police car pulled me over.

Two coppers got out, checked my details and informed me that there was a motoring warrant out for my arrest.

Fuck off I thought. I haven't done anything wrong. This must be a mistake. The coppers knew who I was and we were chatting idly about football as they radioed back to their station for advice.

They didn't seem too concerned and neither was I. It would be sorted out in a few minutes and I'd be on my way.

I'd bent a few rules as a kid. I'd driven without passing my test when I was younger. I bought a car at the age of 20 as soon as I earned some good money (mainly because I could and it was expected of young and successful people to have some flash wheels where I came from) and drove for about a year unlicensed and without insurance or tax.

It got the the point where I had became paranoid and I realised this was something I should not have been doing, this forced me to take driving lessons and I passed my test two months later.

Anyway, I surely hadn't been stopped because of that? As I was talking to the police I could hear the person on the other end of the radio mention 'triggering cameras' and then it hit me what was going on.

Towards the end of my time at Coventry and the beginning of my year at Charlton I'd set a few speed cameras off while driving near my Northampton home. The summonses came through which was obviously a pain and a hassle for me, but a guy I knew said he had someone on the inside at the DVLA who could make the fines disappear.

~ MR FIX IT ~

This bloke was a well-known fixer for footballers. Wherever the London-based footballers were, this guy was alongside them, so I used him.

He didn't ask for anything in return. I did give him a couple of match tickets, but I never heard anything about the six speeding tickets I'd collected so I assumed they'd been dealt with.

I was in a bad place mentally at the time of the offences. Normally, I'd have accepted the tickets, took the points and paid the fines. It wasn't as though I couldn't afford it, but thinking straight was not a habit of mine at that time.

I didn't want to lose my licence as that would have made my life even worse than it was. It was pretty bad at that time.

So being pulled over now had to be as a result of that. There were no other skeletons in my cupboard.

It was hardly crime of the century though so I was confident it would all be sorted out in a couple of hours. Instead it dragged on for a couple of days, and as it turned out that was only the start of it.

I was formally arrested and taken to Bethnal Green Police Station, but I had to wait there for the police from Northampton to come and pick me up.

The whole situation was laughable. If they had my details on file, which obviously they did, why on earth didn't the Northampton police come and see me at my Northampton home?!

It was all a big joke which the police at Bethnal Green also found funny. Anyway, two policemen from Northampton finally arrived at 8pm (about 10 hours after I'd been arrested) and drove me to Weston Favell police station.

I'd been in the cell all fucking day. I had a splitting headache by now and my mind was racing about all over the place. That's never a good situation with my background.

I coped by convincing myself that the offences were so trivial and had taken place so long ago that I'd get a telling off and be on my way. That's if anyone ever got, round to questioning me.

The police looking after me were fine. They let me call Sofia and my dad. I explained to them that I was in a bit of trouble, that they shouldn't worry about it as it wasn't that serious, but it would probably be a good idea to get a lawyer ready in Northampton for me just in case.

All the way back to Northampton these two coppers, who also knew me, were hammering their superiors, in between the usual football chat, for sending them all that way just to pick a suspect up over a few speeding tickets.

It seemed to me that the rank and file coppers were okay, but they had issues with their superiors for following procedure rigidly rather than employing common sense.

It was late when we reached Weston Favell and the detective in charge of the case wasn't around so I was shoved in another cell overnight. I was getting edgy now and predictably I couldn't sleep.

It was now dawning on me that I could be in more trouble than I realised. Spending a night in a cell was one of the worst experiences of my life.

It's the not knowing what's going on that gets you. I didn't believe I had done too much wrong, but did the police share that opinion? The longer I was in that cell the more I feared the worst.

It was freezing cold, I was lying on a rock hard bench, my head was thumping and I was alone. Feeling lonely was dangerous for someone with my history and I don't mind admitting that I was scared.

Guilty or innocent there was not a cat in hell's chance that I would ever put myself in this position again.

My isolation was interrupted once. In the middle of the night a DC Coles opened the slit on my door and asked if I knew why I was there? And had I heard of a garage called Pembur Motors based in South London? I answered no to both questions and thought nothing more of it.

Pembur Motors meant nothing to me. Maybe Mr Fixit owned it.

~ YELLOW CARD ~

My lawyer arrived and I was interviewed the next morning, but it was obvious to everyone in the room that I wasn't a criminal. The lawyer knew it, DC Coles knew it and his sergeant, knew it.

Sure, I'd done something stupid by letting a third party take care of my speeding tickets, but no-one had been hurt.

Anyway, I answered every question truthfully and politely. I admitted to the speeding offences and admitted to trying to make them go away.

I was apologetic and embarrassed that I'd acted as I did. My head had been in a really bad place at the time, but I didn't offer that as an excuse as I just wanted to get out of there.

I refused to name the man with the supposed DVLA contact as we didn't grass people up where I come from, but they knew so much about the case I assumed they'd find him themselves.

I am confident they knew his name, but I have no idea why they have never arrested him.

What this guy had done was to create letters from a fictional garage he called Pembur Motors saying my car was in for a service or an MOT at the times of the speeding offences so there must have been a mistake made by the cameras.

My head was still in a mess at that point in my life. I wasn't acting rationally, but I didn't actually make all that shit up, that was the other guy.

It was a crazy story and you'd have to be pretty stupid to think it could ever work. The letters to the police were so amateurish, Inspector Clouseau would have seen through them.

DC Coles said he believed me and wanted to give me a caution. He went away and his sergeant clearly agreed so they offered me the caution and I accepted it without hesitation.

It was the first time I'd been cautioned by the police since I'd been involved in a fight as a 13 year-old. I did bend the rules now and again, but I was no law-breaker.

When I finally left the station, I was buzzing. I was so relieved to get out of there. Being banged up in a shitty little cell overnight had been a total nightmare.

It wasn't just how uncomfortable physically you become, but fear of the immediate future builds up gradually, another dangerous thought process for someone like me.

Any charge against me would get in the papers and embarrass my family and that thought horrified me. I'm a well-known footballer so there would have been no chance of this being swept under the carpet.

All my personal shit would be dragged into the public domain if this got to court.

I tell you the feeling as I left the station with 'only' a caution matched the feeling of when I scored for Norwich against Manchester United.

It was relief rather than excitement this time, but I was euphoric. I signed for Northampton Town a week later so I was back on track.

Or so I thought......

~ CHARGED NOT CAUTIONED ~

About five months later, I was chilling at home one afternoon. Life was cool. I was going okay at Northampton. Me and Sofia were happy.

My calm was disturbed by a knock on the door. Two police officers were stood there. Both were stern-faced, miserable fuckers who announced that my case regarding six speeding tickets and a fraudulent attempt to avoid paying them had been reviewed and that the top brass weren't happy with the caution I'd received.

This was a caution I had accepted five months earlier. That business was finished as far as I was concerned. I'd had a scare that would stop me offending again. I wouldn't even drop litter in the street for fear of being banged up in a police cell for another night.

But these two cops didn't care about any of that. They claimed the caution should never have been authorised and they'd passed the details on to the Crown Prosecution Service (CPS) who wanted to charge me with perverting the course of justice, an offence that could mean 18 months in prison.

Bearing in mind the actual speeding offences were now two years old this again made no sense. It crossed my mind that a high-profile court case perhaps attracted the bigwigs at the police and the CPS.

The police searched my house. They took all my computer stuff and lots of private correspondence as they were looking for proof that I had written the letters that were supposed to have come from the fictitious garage.

The letters had been written in terrible English. I couldn't have written them that badly if I'd tried and the handwriting on some other bits of evidence bore no resemblance to mine either, while the language used just wouldn't have come from my head.

The computer was returned six months later with casual confirmation that nothing incriminating had been found. No apology for the disruption came with it though.

The police even had a warrant for Sofia's arrest as they suspected she had aided me in my crimes and they questioned her and suggested other high profile footballers were suspected of doing the same thing.

They told Sofia some names of players they believed had also used the same 'Mr Fix It' to see if they could get a reaction from her. Sofia didn't recognise anyone, but she told me some of the names that were mentioned and I did know a few.

When I saw one of the players on the list, I gave him a head-ups and he jumped on a plane and left the country.

I don't think, the police hadn't managed to catch anyone else and it felt like they were taking their frustrations out on me. They were trying to make me nervous by coming to my house, taking my stuff away and interviewing my wife.

I realised I was in big trouble now. I bumped into 'Mr Fix It' once and told him I couldn't go down for him, but he just mumbled that he'd sort it and predictably I never heard from him again.

My lawyers tried to get the case thrown out for an abuse of process, based on the fact that the original offences were so old and the fact that I'd already been cautioned.

We were back in court in November 2011, by which time I'd now joined Kettering, to argue our case.

It seemed to me like we had a pretty strong argument. My legal team certainly thought so and as far as I could see we were being hounded because of a technicality and because I was a high profile offender.

My Barrister, Charles Langley, argued my case strongly in court as we tried to get these six counts of perverting the course of justice thrown out.

The court heard that I had provided false documents on six occasions between February 2008 and December 2009 in an attempt to avoid responsibility for speeding tickets generated by fixed speed cameras.

The documents claimed that mechanics had been working on the car on each occasion so the speed cameras must have been mistaken.

They were all facts, but Langley protested that I had been unfairly prejudiced by the offer of a police caution, which after all is an admission of guilt. It simply wasn't fair that I was charged again with the same offence five months later.

Apparently, the police officers who dealt with the case in the first place, had no right to make the decision to issue a caution.

A newspaper article at the time reported that Langley said in court: "Detective Constable Simon Coles and Detective Sergeant Gez Jackson talked to each other and decided it wasn't a very serious case and offered him the caution.

"It was only when their colleague, the investigating officer Detective Sergeant Andy Blaize, came back to work the next day that their error was noticed.

"Mr McKenzie left the police station that day believing he was a free man. He made plans for his life. At the time he was playing for Northampton Town and now he plays for Kettering.

"However when the summons arrived he could not get a new contract as no football club would touch him with a barge pole because he could go to jail.

"It would have been different if the police realised their error as soon as he left and phoned him when he was outside the station, but it was a full five months before Mr McKenzie was notified of the police error."

I learnt in court that as perverting the course of justice is a serious offence, the decision on whether to caution or go to court was a matter for the Crown Prosecution Service not the police.

That's fair enough, but it wasn't my mistake so therefore it shouldn't have been my problem. The fact also still remained that these offences had taken place two years ago. The fact still remained that I'd held my hands up at the first opportunity and the fact still remained that basically I'd given speeding points to someone else, a common occurrence and not one that usually ended with a court case and prison sentence.

The police lawyer even admitted that certain members of the police force could and should have done better, but that the charges were so serious they had to be re-instated.

She didn't have too much passion in her speech, unlike my barrister.

Judge Richard Bray listened intently to all this legal speak and decided he would take time over his decision.

A few days later, he returned and decided he didn't have the power to quash the caution (good news for me) and he berated the police for their habit of issuing cautions for serious crimes that should blatantly have gone to court (not good for me).

Bray moaned that cautions had become popular with the police as they save time, effort and expense compared to investigating and pursuing crime properly.

But crucially he admitted that, although he couldn't quash the caution, the High Court in London could and now it was up to the

CPS to decide whether or not they wanted to pursue that option. They did and the High Court agreed with them. My caution was removed from my record and now I realised I had a serious problem.

I'd pleaded guilty when accepting the caution so there was little point in pleading not guilty now so I was totally at the mercy of the courts.

I was facing a prison sentence, or as virtually everyone involved in the case predicted, a fine and a ticking off.

A court date was set for four months later. I was left to stew in my own thoughts until then.

CHAPTER 5

'I WANTED TO KNOCK THIS MANAGER OUT'

I was playing for Northampton Town in League Two when the police came knocking on my door.

I enjoyed it at Sixfields at first. To be honest I was just happy to be playing after the suicide attempt and the original nonsense with the police.

I was grateful for the opportunity given to me by manager Ian Sampson. My problems at that club started when Sampson left and Gary Johnson replaced him.

I knew from our first meeting that I wasn't going to get on with Johnson.

He was a little shit towards me. I think it was like He had 'little-man' syndrome and, in my opinion, he was a bully who made crap decisions, I felt that his coaching sessions weren't up to scratch and he blamed the players.

Nothing was ever Johnson's fault. It didn't take him long to lose the entire dressing room and he never really got it back.

To be honest, when he was appointed the players thought he'd be okay. We realised he'd struggled in his last job at Peterborough, but he had done well at Yeovil and Bristol City and he should have been just what we needed in our battle to stay in the Football League.

I'd played against his City teams and they were usually well organised and hard to beat. Anyway I didn't do pre-conceptions about anyone as I liked to take people as I found them.

Personally, at that stage of my career I needed a manager who understood how to get the best out of me.

Someone who knew how to treat me right, with respect for what I'd done at a good level in the past and for what I could still do.

To be frank, short of Steve Coppell turning up at Sixfields, that was unlikely to happen, but if Johnson turned out to be good for the club then I wouldn't be a problem for him.

I'd respect anyone as long as they respected me. I was at that time playing for a struggling League Two team whose Football League future was at risk, but my career had involved Premier League football and that should have counted for something.

My expectations dipped from that first meeting though. Johnson called the first-team into the dressing room. Most of the players sat down, but I stood up as there were no spare seats, and he walked around shaking everyone's hand.

He missed me out. He later claimed that it was an accident and that he hadn't seen me, but I felt he was making a point to the whole squad. It was as if even though he didn't know me, he wanted to show that big-name players meant nothing to him.

I soon found out that Johnson had spoken with the coaches and other management staff before he met the players.

Stuart our physio, a bloke who I got on really well with, had told Johnson about my knee problems and that I couldn't train every day. If I did my knee would swell up and then I'd be of no use to anyone.

Johnson didn't like that. His attitude was that if I didn't train I wouldn't play, but he never said that to my face.

I'm a good reader of people. I was now very uncomfortable at this club. I didn't like this man and I didn't like his brother, who had arrived with him as a scout but it wasn't clear to me what he actually did.

My pride had been hurt. I was top scorer at the club and now I'd been removed from the first-team plans. I couldn't understand it and the rest of the squad were baffled so I was sure the fans would also have been pretty surprised.

I didn't think much of Johnson's ability to manage people. It seemed to me that he made bad decisions, but worse than that, he most of the time he didn't take responsibility for them.

He'd blurt on about giving youth a chance as an excuse for even leaving me off the substitutes' bench, but nothing he tried worked. Our results were dreadful and morale was at rock-bottom.

We hadn't been winning many games when Johnson turned up, but we had been difficult to beat. We still couldn't win after he started work, but we did become a lot easier to beat!

We lost his first three games in charge and I wasn't involved in any of them, not even as a substitute. We managed a couple of draws and then I sneaked onto the bench, but I was playing 10 minutes here and five minutes there so I wasn't getting much of a chance to influence matches.

Johnson fancied himself as a wise guy, an expert in amateur psychology, but whatever mental games he thought he was practising it was as shit as his management. Rubbishing players in public was never a sensible tactic at any club, never mind one with already little confidence in the dressing room.

Johnson also brought loads of players to the club who were no better than those already there. We all joked that he must be getting a cut of the transfer deals as some of the players were just so average, which was not what we needed in our position. He wasn't of course, but he clearly had no clue as to how to get this side away from the bottom of the table.

The spirit was so bad, and the results so awful, that relegation from the Football League was becoming a serious prospect.

Eventually, Johnson must have run out of ideas and options because he sent me on at half-time in a Good Friday game against Rotherham at Sixfields.

We were 2-0 down at half-time so Johnson was clearly desperate when I was sent on and I got us back into the game with a goal before Liam Davis equalised in the last minute.

My goal was only a tap-in after a goalmouth scramble, but I celebrated like I'd scored at Wembley. That was me saying 'fuck you' at Johnson.

I could have been scoring goals for weeks and if I had we wouldn't all be in this position. Handled correctly I was capable of getting my goals and helping the team.

The rest of the lads knew my feelings and so did Johnson. He pulled me in training the next week, told me I was starting the next match, which if we won would guarantee us staying up, and he was friendly towards me for a couple of weeks.

Johnson started letting me miss training sessions, but I just found his whole approach embarrassing. If he'd treated me like that from the start and showed me some respect we'd have got on fine and I would have scored the goals that kept us out of trouble. I never thought I was a special case just because I was an ex-Premier League player now playing in League Two, but it wasn't rocket science to work out how to get the best out of me.

Despite the late-season thaw in our relationship, it was too late for him to salvage it completely. I started the next game at Stockport, but came off injured after half an hour, after creating a goal, and then missed the last couple of games through injury.

We drew at Stockport 2-2, but won the last two matches against Stevenage and Morecambe to ensure our safety.

They were the only two games we won with Johnson in charge that season. That record backs up my opinion that he was a terrible manager for Northampton.

It wasn't just me who didn't like or trust him though. Shaun Harrod was a decent striker with a good scoring record in the lower divisions, but Johnson used to single him out for criticism. According to Johnson, Shaun never made the right runs, he was never in the right place and he couldn't shoot straight. Johnson was always at him.

After another defeat Johnson lost it completely and charged up to Shaun in the dressing room shouting 'you've never shown me a fucking thing, you're a complete waste of fucking time.'

It was quite funny to see this little bloke trying to get physical. He was lucky Shaun was a placid bloke and didn't try and hit him back.

I wish Johnson had tried that shit on me. I'd have clocked him if he ever treated me in this way.

Shaun was just embarrassed by what had happened but his self-esteem was knocked for six. I spent a few weeks helping to build his confidence back up as the manager apparently couldn't be bothered. He was too a good a player to be destroyed by the rantings of someone I viewed as a muppet.

During Johnson's time at Northampton, I was in and out of court, but he never once spoke to me about my situation. He showed no sympathy and expressed no concern whereas his predecessor Ian Sampson wrote a letter on my behalf to the judge in my case.

I wasn't making a song and dance about my problems, but Johnson must have known what I was going through. A word of encouragement here and there would have been appreciated, but he showed no interest in the welfare of a player who could have been useful to him.

As I missed the end of the season, Johnson started ignoring me again. I was no use to him now so I didn't exist as far he was concerned.

I was disgusted by him and his treatment of me before the last game of the season tipped me over the edge. I now wanted to fight him.

On the Friday before the game my son Kasey was mugged for the few quid he had on him on his way home from school. He was 14. Kasey was distressed so I belonged by his side and I went to Norwich on a Friday to see him. I told Stuart, the physio, what had happened and left him to tell Johnson that I might be late for the match as I'd probably stay in Norwich overnight.

I wasn't playing so it shouldn't have been a big deal, but I then received a message from someone at the club telling me Johnson wanted me to stay away from the ground altogether. The exact words relayed to me were 'tell him to stay the fuck away'.

Was he punishing me for my son getting mugged? It certainly felt like it. How dare he talk to me like that? Everyone knew that I would drop everything if my kids needed me and yet this man was seemingly belittling me for going to help my only son.

I was now raging inside and I still wanted to support the team. By the time I arrived at the ground, I knew I was going to knock this man out.

Word must have got out that I was after Johnson as one of our coaches Tim Flowers was waiting for me in the club car park when I arrived.

He physically restrained me and asked me not to disrupt the team's preparations. He told me later he could see the anger in my eyes and that he was frightened even though I had no beef with him.

I assured him I wouldn't let things kick off, but I still went into the dressing in order to embarrass Johnson.

I strolled in, stared at this little twat in a penguin suit, and let him know just by looking at him what I thought of him as a man as well as a manager.

I was challenging him to repeat what he'd said about telling me to stay away from the ground, but he didn't have the bottle. He didn't say a word to me. I was telling him that I didn't respect his authority just by defying his orders and standing there in his dressing room.

I knew I wouldn't get another contract at Northampton, but Johnson had to see the players individually to tell them who was staying and who was leaving and I couldn't wait for my chance.

I was still steaming two weeks after the season ended when it was my turn to see him. I burst in, slammed the door behind me and laid into Johnson while his brother looked on, doing and saying nothing.

'Why did you disrespect me behind my back?' I demanded to know. 'Why did you slag me off to the coaches?' 'Why, from the day you walked into the club, did you treat me like I was one of your kids rather than a player with 10 years experience of the Football League? What exactly was your problem with me?'

Johnson stuttered and stammered some unconvincing rubbish, in my opinion and eventually got round to telling me that I wasn't getting a new contract, but I wasn't bothered about that. I also wanted to know why he'd sent abusive messages through someone else, as opposed to coming to me.

Johnson predictably denied that last accusation, but it was pretty obvious to me that the person involved wouldn't make something like that up.

Johnson offered to call that person up to his office, so I called his bluff and agreed, but it never happened.

Johnson was spineless. He was incapable of fronting up. In my opinion he was forever bluffing and I had caught him out on this occasion.

My Northampton journey was over though. I did ring Johnson a couple of months later to see if I could train with the team in pre-season to keep fit, but not surprisingly he wouldn't entertain that.

He flannelled for a bit, claimed that I'd be a distraction, but I just put the phone down on him and started looking elsewhere for help.

I suppose it was a bit optimistic of me! Johnson clearly knew that I didn't rate him as a manager or as a man and I assume that he knew I didn't like him as a person at all.

He probably reckoned that I might poison some of the other players, but to be honest I wouldn't have done that as that would have disrespected him after he'd finally shown me some kindness.

Alan Smith was a show off and a terrible manager at Crystal Palace when I was there, but Johnson was much worse. In my opinion, he was a sneaky, divisive figure and I wasn't at all surprised when he was sacked by Northampton a few weeks into the next season.

It was a shame my Northampton career ended so badly. They took me on after I'd received my police caution.

Sampson signed me. After training with Northampton for a

couple of weeks, he offered me a year's contract on a salary that meant I could pay my mortgage and my other bills, basically because he remembered me terrorising him when he played for Northampton and I played for Peterborough.

He told me I was brilliant that day (we both scored in that game at London Road, but his was the winner) and he made me want to play for him just by being so positive. I was drained with all the time I'd wasted with the police and I wasn't in the best of shape, but he made me want to play again.

The season had already started when I went there. The team didn't start the season well and hadn't won a game when I was given my home debut in a match against Southend.

I didn't play great, but it was just good to be out on the pitch again and even better to be in a dressing room sharing the banter.

We won that game 2-1, but the winning goal arrived after I'd gone off midway through the second-half.

I was enjoying it though. There was a good team spirit and it was a happy dressing room.

I managed 90 minutes of the next game, a defeat at Shrewsbury before I was back on the bench for a few weeks even though we were on a bit of a losing run.

I finally got my chance again in a big bottom of the table clash against Hereford at home and what a game that turned out to be, on a personal and a team level.

I was on fire. I hadn't felt this sharp, this lively and this fit for ages. At half-time we were 3-0 up and I had scored the lot.

I was buzzing, the team was buzzing and the fans were enjoying a rare bit of success and a very good team performance. We were happy in the home dressing room during the interval without being complacent.

I don't know what was said in the Hereford dressing room at half-time, but they came out kicking everything that moved and a few things that didn't.

Sampson soon hauled me off as he wanted me fit and fresh for the next game. I didn't have a problem with that so I accepted the applause of the crowd and headed off down the tunnel for a shower.

About 20 minutes later, I was walking back up the tunnel and all I could hear was boos and jeers from our fans. They were screaming blue murder and no wonder because Hereford had turned the game on its head and were now winning 4-3.

I couldn't believe it and I felt for Sampson as he was copping plenty of flak. To be fair to the manager though, he wasn't the only one who thought we had the game won at half-time.

We had decent players like Liam Davis and Abdul Osman, but mentally we were weak. That result was a real blow to Sampson and although he survived a few more months his card had been marked in my opinion.

I actually scored in three of the next four matches and we even managed to win a couple of them, but we were just treading water as a team.

We were just winning the odd game here and there to keep ourselves out of trouble. I scored the winner in a big derby game at home to Oxford and an equaliser in a bruising game at Port Vale.

But we went on a run of seven games without a win and our position was looking a bit perilous to say the least.

After a 3-2 defeat at home to Burton when we were 3-0 down after 40 minutes, Sampson was sacked.

I felt sorry for him. The players hadn't performed for him and he didn't deserve that as he was a good bloke, unlike the man who replaced him.

I scored 10 goals that season, but I was ready to jack it when Johnson released me.

Kettering Town then came in for me. Offered me a decent deal for that standard of football for a year and I thought I'd give it another season.

I loved football banter, I loved scoring goals, but I didn't enjoy not getting paid which is what happened at Kettering.

They were a shambles. The manager was a lovely bloke called

Morrell Maison. He looked like comedian Bernie Mac and had as much idea about football as well.

We were playing at Rushden & Diamonds so the crowds were poor and it was soon obvious that the club had no money.

It was like a fucking circus. No-one would know who was going to turn up and play from one week to the next.

We were playing Gateshead away one Saturday and we met at the ground early in the morning (overnight stays were a no-no) to be greeted by a bus which looked like it had been driven to the ground straight from the 1930s.

It was small, dirty and we would be in it for a round-trip of eight hours to play at a stadium with an athletics track all the way around the pitch.

We actually drew 1-1 and I scored, which just about saved it from being the most miserable day of my entire career.

Now I loved football, but this was tough. I'd played in the Premier League not that long ago, but this couldn't be much further removed. I knew then my stay at Kettering was not going to last.

Kettering stopped paying the players soon afterwards, so I became an unofficial shop steward for the squad, because I was the most experienced and because I was the bolshiest.

We had lads with mortgages and kids who couldn't put petrol in the car. Kettering used to moan about the size of the contracts the players were on, but as they'd offered the contracts in the first place it wasn't much of an argument.

Maison left and Mark Stimson replaced him. He was a quality coach, but the financial situation just worsened and players were leaving on a daily basis as their contracts weren't being honoured. The club wanted the players to tear up their contracts and accept new, much worse ones. It went on for months, we'd get paid in dribs and drabs and in the end I did rip mine up and retired from football.

My farewell game was against Bath at home on December 17. I invited all my friends and family to the match and to be fair to the club they put on a good day for me.

Stimson said some lovely words before and after the game about me. We drew 1-1 in front of a crowd of just over 1,000 so it was a good job I'd invited so many people!

I didn't score, but I was happy enough to draw the curtain on my career. This wasn't how I envisaged it ending, but I had bigger things to deal with now.

I was between the court case and the sentencing for a start. After that was over, I wanted to get on with supporting my family as well as footballers who were suffering like I had suffered.

Kettering owed me about £6,000, but I took £1500 and walked away.

It was sad to see the club just keep lurching from crisis to crisis and they were badly let down by their chairman.

As soon as I saw Ladak parading Paul Gascoigne as Kettering manager a few years earlier I suspected the club might end up in trouble one day.

It's a crying shame especially for the fans who supported what had been one of the top non-league clubs in the country.

CHAPTER 6

'RAGE AGAINST THE SYSTEM'

February 21, 2012 was my final day in court and the signs weren't good from the start.

Judge Richard Bray looked very pleased with himself at Northampton Crown Court. He was about to pass judgement on a well-known footballer so it was a chance for him to look tough. This dark cloud had been hanging over my head for two years. For the last six months of that, I'd been in and out of court fighting six counts of perverting the course of justice over the failure to pay a few speeding tickets.

Now I'm not saying I was above the law, but I definitely learnt my lesson one night in a police station a year earlier. That wasn't an experience I would ever be in a hurry to repeat.

I'd failed to have the case thrown out despite some stupid police bungling and now I was at the mercy of one man.

Judge Bray listened to my character witnesses, but his expression didn't change. He was stony-faced when we first saw him and he remained that way now.

When the legal niceties were over and my witnesses had had their say, he didn't waste any time.

He left no room for any hope for me and my supporters who had packed out the court.

"A custodial sentence is necessary for this type of offence which strikes right at the heart of justice," Bray boomed.

"It would completely send out the wrong message if I did not hand out a custodial sentence.

I give you credit for your early guilty plea and I am aware that you were suffering at the time from depression, but you have committed a professional fraud by pretending that your car was in a garage that didn't exist and I cannot excuse you completely. You will go to prison for six months."

In an instant my life had been shattered again.

I was to spend three months in prison (half the sentence is normal). I was also given an 18-month driving ban.

My brilliant and credible witnesses hadn't made a difference, and nor had my illness.

Incredibly when we were fighting against the case even coming to court Bray had appeared to be on my side.

He had found it ridiculous that the police seemed to be arguing amongst themselves about the merits of the case.

Now Bray had decided that a wife and four young kids (baby Talia had by now been born) could live without their devoted, loving husband and father because of something that happened two years previously.

He'd condemned me to prison, a category A prison at that, as my family crumbled and sat roaring their eyes out, comforted by my friends who just looked stunned.

My sister and mum were hysterical. I sat there bemused, holding back the tears, but raging inside at the injustice of it all.

I'd been through so much. I'd tried to commit suicide once before so what possible good could it do to send me to prison on two year-old offences that had been committed when I was in such a bad place?

That's not an excuse for my actions, but it was the first time I'd ever been in trouble in my whole professional life.

I could have received a suspended sentence or community service (unpaid work they call it now) because of my background and previous good record.

I may as well have been on a different planet back then. I was certainly now a different person and it just baffled me that the prosecutors and the judge couldn't see that. After all, these offences had harmed absolutely no-one but myself and my own family.

The more I thought about it, the more I felt it was all bollocks. The law is so inconsistent. I read about repeat offenders getting suspended sentences, but I had committed my first 'crime' and I was to end up inside.

I have no respect at all for the system. Some of the police were top people, but some are a joke and they shouldn't be pursuing people like me. They should be after the murderers, the drugs dealers and the rapists not people committing their first offences. I was told that one judge was likely to send you away for five years while another would just rap you on the knuckles for the same offence, but surely something as serious as prison shouldn't be determined by a judge's mood on one particular day?

I wasn't one of those arrogant footballers who showed no remorse after being caught doing something bad. I didn't believe I was above the law. On the contrary, I was mortified by my behaviour and, although my illness was a mitigating factor, I didn't try and use it to exonerate my actions completely.

I pleaded guilty from the start after being advised that would lead to a mere caution. I'd expressed regret and I was happy to take my punishment on the chin, but a prison sentence, for something that had happened over two years ago and for which I'd already been punished?

That would be so far over-the-top for my case it was just ludicrous. The amount of good wishes I received from people on both sides of the process convinced me I was right.

The night before sentencing I had a great group of people round my house in Northampton.

Best-selling rapper MC Harvey (or just plain Harvey as I knew him), someone I'd known since my teens and who had helped me push my music career, was there as was Michael Duberry, one of my closest friends, while my cousin Damien McKenzie, a source of great support for me throughout my life, was also about.

To see high profile people like that, showing their support in a very public as well as private way was humbling. Harvey dropped his busy lifestyle to be by my side as we went to court guaranteeing his picture would be in the paper the next day alongside someone in my situation.

None of us present that night could believe I'd get sent down for speeding offences that were several years old. It wasn't just a case of my people keeping my spirits high, it really was what we all truly believed.

I knew from talking to people, that the junior ranks at Northampton police didn't think I should end up in prison.

Amid all the heart to hearts that took place that night, we all agreed there's no way that a bus driver would be prosecuted for what I'd done.

The police and the prosecutors, in my opinion wanted to make an example of a high profile figure and they'd done that already by taking me to a public court in the first place.

It was bound to be in the papers now and they could all look tough. They had no need to take it any further with a prison sentence.

The night before sentencing I didn't sleep a wink. Sleepless nights had been a common occurrence in the last few years, but I steered clear of sleeping pills now.

Mum turned up the next morning with my step-dad, dad and sister. It was emotional and I felt for them having to watch their first-born child go through this ordeal.

If they were angry with me they hid it well. They backed me as they always had done, but the guilt of putting them through three tough years still haunts me now.

Mum promised me everything would be fine because that's what mums do. Dad was a rock as always. 'You're going to be okay Champ,' he'd insist. 'No matter what happens you will come through this because you have fight in your blood.'

I believed him. I wanted to believe him at least.

We drove to court. This was the most nerve-wracking moment of my life. I'd played in big pressure football matches, but I could control what happened on those occasions because of my ability. This was different. I couldn't do any more. I'd done all I could by accepting responsibility for my actions and my legal people had fought as hard as they could to keep me away from this moment. The press were waiting for us on the courthouse steps. TV cameras and newspaper photographers were blazing away from the minute they saw us.

We barged through without saying a word. We went to the court and waited for Judge Bray to appear.

I had some good people come and speak up for me in court.

Clarke Carlisle of the PFA (the professional footballers union were by now actively involved in helping footballers cope with depression) spoke up for me. He explained about all the good work I was now doing, with players suffering what I had suffered. Clarke also tried to explain my condition and how it would have affected my decision-making at the time of the offences.

My uncle Duke, an MBE, spoke brilliantly about what pressure can do to professional sportsmen. He too said he'd suffered bouts of depression because the ups and downs of sport at the highest level could be difficult to balance.

Duke said: "People think we live in these glamorous lifestyles, but we're under the same pressures as everyone else. The pressure builds up if things are not going your way."

Northampton manager Ian Sampson sent in a glowing character reference as did former Norwich star Darren Eadie, a player I now help with problems similar to mine.

Everyone who spoke insisted sending a man with depression to prison would do no-one any good. I was a man of previously good character who was hardly likely to re-offend.

Judge Richard Bray took a different veiw.

"I can do three months, I can do that," I was telling myself more in hope than expectation as I sat there waiting to be led away.

I released the following statement on Twitter as I was sent down. It was aimed at my friends, family and supporters.

"I prepared this statement to be able to share with you all how I am feeling and most of all to explain what happened.

"A few years ago I was not in a good place and couldn't always make sense of what was going on. Some things being personal and some being work related.

"Unfortunately at that time I fell deep into depression which led me to try and take my life.

"Around that period I wasn't thinking straight and got caught up with the wrong people around me.

"My behaviour towards certain things like these speeding offences was totally unacceptable and it was very naive of me to allow a third party to take my points for me.

"I allowed someone to take my points innocently, not knowing the seriousness of what was actually happening.

"My mindset at the time was confused and not like it is now. Allowing someone to take my points from me was very stupid of me and I only wish I had been in a better place back then and that I could turn back the clock.

"These offences happened two years ago. I was arrested over a year ago and had been told by the police at the time of my arrest that if I answered all questions, told the truth and gave them everything they needed to know I would be cautioned and not charged.

"I did all that was asked of me and as a result I was given a caution.

"It was only when I was arrested that I really understood just how serious this was. I was cautioned and given a chance to start to get my life back again, which I did and I learnt from my mistakes.

"Five months after receiving the caution, I was told that the police officers who were in charge at the time had made a mistake and that I would now be facing charges.

"The officer in charge reversed the decision and got the caution removed. Two years on I am left with being charged with these offences.

"I broke the law six times in that two-year period which I am now aware of. I am truly sorry for these offences that I committed.

"I must stress to you all, I was not representing the real me back then and I now realise how stupid I have been.

"As most of you, especially the people who really know me are aware, I have been in a better place recently and I have really turned my life around.

"It took a lot to speak out publicly about trying to end my life and now turning it around with helping others with issues of depression and starting a new career in music.

"I feel I have given back in a lot of ways and will continue to do so as soon as I possibly can.

"Anyone reading this, I hope you take note and learn by my mistakes, especially if you are in a bad place with depression.

"I ask anyone with depression to speak out to someone before you start making the same mistakes I did.

"I am not the Leon I was a few years ago. I didn't set the right example and I'm truly sorry for that.

"I believe now that I am Leon, not the Leon I was during that two-year period, my only comment is that I wasn't well at that particular time and was not thinking in a way that I am now.

"I allowed a third party to take points without realising the extent and impact it would cause to me and my family's lives today.

"I am now leaving my wife and my beautiful four children along with some fantastic friends and family. God willing they will be okay.

"Anyone who knows me, knows my heart and more importantly knows the change in me from where I was compared to where I am now.

"I am a fighter and it looks like now I don't have a choice but to battle on which I will do.

"I would like to say a massive thanks to my family and friends for the support they have given me, especially as this has been going on for so long."

It was a message from my heart and it played out well judging by the number of messages of support I received in return.

Many were from people whom I hadn't met and most raged like me about the injustice of my situation.

It was that level of support that I needed now. Prison was waiting for me.

CHAPTER 7

'CHARLES BRONSON AND MYRA HINDLEY'

When Judge Bray passed sentence on me, I didn't look back. I could tell from the tears and the moans that my family were in pieces.

I wanted to join them, but I had to be strong now.

I picked up the bag you're told to prepare in case you get sent down and wandered down the stairs out the back of the court.

I was still in the smart suit I'd selected for the court appearance. I was searched, handcuffed and sat down on a bench inside a container on the prison van that was going to take me to Woodhill Prison, a category A facility where, me, a first-time driving offender, would be mixing with paedophiles, murderers, rapists and other hardcore villains.

I was told Woodhill was a very high security 'Close Supervision Centre' for prisoners who are among the most difficult and disruptive in the prison system.

I don't know what those in the justice system had been told about me then. Maybe they had me confused with some-one else. Maybe Youssef Safri or one of the other footballers I'd had disagreements with had tipped them off that I was a bad lad!

But basically I was a footballer not a criminal. There's no way I deserved to be banged up in prison and no way that I should be sent to such a high security facility.

The guards at the court were sympathetic. The lady whose job it was to explain what would now happen to me, said she couldn't believe that I'd been sent down.

I was listening, but I couldn't reply because my energy had gone. I was so sure I would get a suspended sentence, I had been stunned into silence by the actual decision of Judge Bray.

Other wrong 'uns sentenced that day piled on the prison van. Some knew who I was. One knew I had made a record with my mate Harvey and started rapping to impress me.

It was a surreal moment listening to a criminal rapping on the way to prison, but it did make me laugh at least.

It helped take my mind off what I was about to experience which I assumed was going to be some sort of living hell.

One night in a police cell had scared me shitless, but at least in there, no physical harm was likely to come my way. A couple of months locked up with what I imagined were pretty evil bastards could be very different.

I've seen plenty of prison movies and walking into Woodhill for the first time felt like being in a film.

The residents were eyeing me up and down, checking me out. Convicts came out of their cells to have a look at the newbies.

Believe it or not some started chanting my name, not in a bad way, but like they were fans watching me play in a football match. 'Leon, Leon, Leon', they shouted. I didn't know whether I was supposed to wave at them or just keep my head down.

But inside I was scared and I knew I couldn't show it. Mentally I was preparing myself for this challenge and showing any sort of weakness was not an option if I was to survive.

I'd been verbally abused by one guy as I walked in for the first time. I clocked his face though and challenged him when I saw him in the gym later. He backed down, I gained some respect.

It was shit at the start though. I was placed on suicide watch because of my background. I was left on my own in a cell with guards checking up on me every hour to make sure I was still breathing.

I felt the situation was completely bizarre. The authorities clearly recognised I had a mental illness and yet they still sent me to a facility that would test tougher minds than mine.

The powers that be couldn't have known it, but there was no danger of a second attempt to top myself though.

This was a massive challenge and I kept thinking back to what life was like for me in the Bexleyheath hotel room. I refused to cry this time, but right now, unlike a couple of years earlier, looking to the future was actually an advantage.

When I was at my lowest, the future was the problem. Now it offered hope, if only I could survive the next three months.

I felt sure I was in a much stronger place mentally and that was thanks in part to the strength of those closest to me and my determination to pursue and realise other dreams.

I'd started helping Clarke Carlisle and the PFA with understanding and helping players suffering from depression and I'd made a record with Harvey to kick-start my music career, something that had appealed to me for years.

Sure, I was miserable and I was still finding it hard to fathom how some stupidity on my part over speeding fines had led me to this situation, but I was determined to stay positive mentally.

The most common question asked in prison, is 'what are you in here for?' Everyone, screws, inmates and office staff fell about laughing when I told them why I was there.

The screws told me Woodhill was a prison that once held Charles Bronson. Fred and Rose West had stayed, Ian Huntley had been an inmate and Myra Hindley had spent time in the women's part. Unit 6 was the place where the most dangerous prisoners were housed.

Bronson apparently had to have six guards accompany him for a pee. He once broke free from his minders just so he could slap the governor in the face so, he clearly relished his reputation as being one of Britain's hardest men.

Bronson described his time at Woodhill as a 'living hell'. He slept on a concrete slab on the floor of a tiny room. His sole window was bullet proof.

Christ, if a nutter like him, who had spent most of his adult life behind bars, found it hard living at Woodhill, how on earth would a pretty footballer like me cope?!

Hindley was the devil incarnate according to the screws. One stare from her made the hairs on the back of the neck stand to attention – she could terrify you without saying a word.

And here I was, Leon McKenzie, family man, following in their footsteps thanks to a lapse in judgement that hadn't hurt anyone apart from me.

Sadly I wasn't even Leon McKenzie any more. I was Prisoner A58 18CL.

I was allowed three visitors a month. I was sentenced on a Wednesday and on the Saturday Sofia and Bruce Dyer, an old Crystal Palace team-mate and long-time friend, came to see me for a couple of hours and, while it was great that I had people who cared for me and loved me enough to want to come and visit me in this place, I didn't let them come back.

I bid a tearful farewell to them both and resigned myself to solitude for the next couple of months.

At visiting times, the prisoners sit there at a table, wearing a bib over their tatty grey prison uniform, waiting for their visitors to come through the door. Emotionally I was wrecked by kids running in to see their prisoner father.

I didn't want my kids to see me in a place like this. Prison was no place for me, never mind my children.

I locked myself away that night and refused to let anyone else visit, until Michael Duberry came in just before I was released.

Sofia told my younger kids that I was away in London working on my music. I spoke to them on the phone occasionally, but hearing my kids' voices made me feel weak. No displays of weakness were recommended in prison.

I missed my baby daughter's first birthday which made me feel like shit. I was constantly in a shitty mood. If anyone had confronted me physically that day I'd have fought them.

~ NASTY NEIGHBOURS ~

The first few days were horrible. The sex offenders, rapists and child abusers were segregated from the rest of us, but they'd walk past me at dinner time and I just wanted to harm them.

The thought of sharing my space with this sort of scum was heart-breaking. I thought that I could never get used to their company. The worst sexual offenders were protected by Rule 45 and it basically defended the rights of rapists and other lowlife. I found it mentally very tough just seeing these slippery fuckers pottering around the joint as though they owned the place, secure in the knowledge that they were the best-protected inmates in the prison.

There was always a temptation to do them some physical damage and I came close once when a mad Irish inmate came into my cell.

He was excited about something and he couldn't wait to tell me that one of the paedos had left his cell door open and that we should go down there and kick the shit out of him.

Honestly, these people were filth and I'd have liked nothing better than to get down there and get stuck in, but there was a voice in my head telling me not to do it. My dad's words about keeping my nose clean inside and to do nothing that would extend my stay inside also helped.

Luckily, these paedos were kept hidden away most of the time and that was the way I preferred it.

Reality kicked in the day after Sofia's visit. My mindset had changed overnight and, even from time in a Category A prison, I had to take what positives I could from being here.

If I could get through this, I could get through anything, even away games at Millwall!

"Tough times don't last, tough people do" is one of my favourite sayings. 'Dubes' reminded me of it in an e-mail he sent (Email A

Prisoner.com is a wonderful service!)

It was the perfect expression for prison and e-mails like this one from 'Dubes' kept me going inside.

'Tough times don't last, but tough people do.

'That best describes both me and you.

'We are good friends, that's the word of others.

'But we both know we would say we are brothers.

'For me, you walked in when many others walked out.

'Neither did you have to scream and shout.

'How will we remember the year we just had?

'Be glad it's over? Will we be happy or sad?

'It's all a lesson, I just hope we pass the test.

'And if there is more of the same, I hope we can avoid the rest.

'You never know how strong you are until being strong is your only choice.

'We are both stronger than we thought and I say that with a confident voice.'

Jason Lee, Bruce Dyer, mum, Sofia, dad, Rebecca, Clarke Carlisle and my cousin Damien all wrote to me as did Spoony, under his real name of Jonathan Joseph.

Me and Spoony have become really good friends since that time and like Dubes said 'many will walk out of your life, but the true friends will walk in.'

Daily Mail Sports Editor Lee Clayton, also wrote me a lovely long letter. He was a bit of a Palace fan and used my dad's gym.

I had a dear friend Sue Gallop who worked behind the scenes at Charlton and she got in touch while I was inside.

I also had notes from well-wishers I didn't know. I thank them all from the bottom of my heart as it was so vital to me to know that so many people from so many different walks of life were on my side.

I print some extracts here.

From SOFIA (wife)

After a visit...

'I felt so close to you today, but yet it also felt so far

'I wish I could come and see you every day.

'I was just about to select a scripture to send you, I opened the bible and it landed on Proverb 31 10c:

(A wife of noble character who can find? She is worth more than rubies.

Her husband has full confidence in her and lacks nothing in value.

She brings him good, not harm, all the days of her life).

'I just want to let you know that I love you with all my heart and that every second of every hour I am thinking of your beautiful face and hoping that you might call so I can hear your voice and have a few moments of calmness and peace!

'You are my all, always have been and no matter what life throws at us, we will get through it like we have always done.'

A letter a month later....

"Hello my beautiful husband.

'It's our baby girl's birthday today and, while I have a few moments to myself, I wanted to write you a card to say 'thank you' for blessing me with two little angels.

'It's amazing that a year has passed since the day she was born. She is a perfect addition to our family and I feel so lucky to have her.

'All your children are fine. Nothing will change

'It's so hard waking up and not having you here, but we are all so proud of you.'

Sofia, Queen B.

From DONNA CHATFIELD (mum)

'Thank you for writing to me, it was wonderful to hear from you even though it brought me to tears.

'I'm glad you're getting to the gym as it's good to keep yourself in shape mentally as well as physically.

'When you feel down or angry you can take it out on the equipment by imagining there's a certain face on it!

'I feel pretty useless because as your mum I should be there to protect you no matter how old you are, but I'm powerless and that hurts.

'We all make mistakes though. We are all human and it's how we deal with those mistakes that will be important.

'No matter what happens or no matter what changes, your family are here for you. We will never leave your side.

'This challenge is the biggest that you have ever faced, but you will succeed as you have succeeded in everything else that you have taken up.

'Keep that chin up'

Mum.

From JOHNATHAN JOSEPH (aka DJ Spoony)

'Yo bro, hope you are well and adjusting to this chapter in your life.

'I know this is going to be a tough period of your life, but these are the things that will define our character.

'You have the fighter sprit in you so call on it when you're not feeling like a top man.

'I can't give you any advice on being away from a partner for so long, but I will say one thing and that is that when you are loved, treasure it.

'Been thinking about some work stuff for you when you get back, turning a negative into a positive, so make the most of your time in there and keep a diary!

'Thinking of you'

Johnathan

From CLARKE CARLISLE (PFA chairman)

'Leon my friend,

'I can only imagine what it's like to be in the position you're in, not just physically, but mentally too.

'I have a real burden of guilt for not helping you enough to get this sentence suspended, but it will be nothing compared to the emotions you're feeling.

'Leon, all who know you, know you have turned your mind and your life around and that it must infuriate you to be where you are for the sins of a past life.

'But know this my friend, every member of your family and every close friend is thinking and praying for you.

'I genuinely believe that this experience will only serve to fuel the fire that is within you, build that passion to help others and add to your ability to make music of substance.

'I want you to know that I am here praying for you and I'll be here when you get out too.

'Sofia is being amazing, so strong and focused. You punched above your weight there big man!

'She is keeping the family unit together for you, all eagerly waiting for you to get home.

'I can't wait for you to hit the streets fella. I really think this is going to galvanise you, help you focus your efforts and clearly define your goals and that excites me!!

'Your new future begins NOW.'

God Bless

Clarke

From BRUCE DYER (friend and former team-mate)

'Hi bro.

'I am lost for words mate, this does not seem real. I believe this madness will work out for your good in the end so this is just a chapter for the book.

'If you can get on some courses and get plugged into the chaplain department at the prison I think it will do you some good.

'We are praying for you. John 6 verse 37: 'All that the father gives me will come to me, and whoever comes to me I will never drive away.'
God bless
Bruce

From LEE CLAYTON (Journalist, family friend)
'I know we don't know each other well enough to be 'friends', but this is not a 'do-good' letter, just a note to say hello and let you know that there are people who care about you and who wish you well.
'I was inspired by your interview with Neil Ashton (Daily Mail journalist) and hope that will give you a platform when you come out to use your story and your troubles as an inspiration to others.
'The PFA need people like you to send out their message and to communicate their personal experiences.
'Your story was a breakthrough moment. It requires great strength to make a difference.
'I hope you are coping with being in prison. I thought your Twitter statement that appeared, as you had intended, the day after your sentencing showed you to be in control of your emotions.
'I hope that is true'
Take care
Lee

From REBECCA MCKENZIE (sister)
'To my handsome, amazing brother.
'It's time to focus on who you really are and how strong your mind is. The stronger you will become of your mind, the stronger you will be when you come home.
'I'm so excited about your music. I know big things are waiting in the pipeline for you.
'You're the first person I think of when I go to sleep and the first

person I think of when I wake up.

'Me and dad play your song every day and dad says you are so special, so talented.

'Be happy'

Rebecca

From JASON LEE (friend and former team-mate)

'Where do I start? Just gutted for you man.

'I know how angry you are and rightly so, but it could have been a lot longer considering this is the same judge that wanted to give you 18 months.

'You can do this time easy. Just keep your head down and do not rise to any bait.

'If you do that you will be back with your family sooner rather than later.

'We'll talk soon my friend.

'Keep fit in mind and body.'

Jason.

~ LEON MCKENZIE – CLEANER ~

I was offered a job as a cleaner which I readily accepted. I served food to the inmates. I had to keep my mind busy and active to get through this. I wrote a journal every day.

Anyway, hoovering earned you extra credits to use on the phone or for chocolate in the canteen so I was happy for once to be doing the household chores.

Believe me, they were huge perks especially as prison meals seemed to consist of starch, potatoes and fried stuff that would sit in your stomach for days.

If you've seen Gordon Ramsey's programme on food in prison, you'll know what it's like. My old Norwich chairman Delia Smith would have been appalled.

I worked hard at my new job. When I was scoring against Manchester United, Man City and Everton in Premier League football, I couldn't have dreamt that I'd be happy mopping floors or serving shit food a few years later, but strangely I was.

Darren Huckerby, a strike partner from my days with Norwich City, had always said I'd do the best job I possibly could whether I was sweeping roads or playing as a striker in the Premier League and he was right, although I'd gone to some extreme lengths to prove it!

I was a good, diligent cleaner and there were perks from being part of the domestic team. I was moved to a slightly bigger cell with 'MCKENZIE – CLEANER' on the door.

Believe me that was a much sought after title inside, even by some of the hard men.

Only problem was I had to share the cell with another member of the cleaning staff, a GBH offender called Wayne.

This concerned me. I did my homework on him. He had obviously been violent, but I was ready for that. I could look after myself if he tried any funny business, so I was more concerned about whether or not he had BO – there's nothing worse than sharing a confined space with someone with personal hygiene problems.

I met Wayne and thankfully he smelt fine. We chatted carefully, cautiously without giving too much away. He said he'd been done for three different cases for fighting, but he said he'd been unlucky, that he'd just been in the wrong place at the wrong time. We spoke about films. 'Man on Fire starring Denzil Washington is one of my favourites,' I told him.

He had a couple of favourites as well. This supposedly violent tough nut said he loved Willy Wonka and the Chocolate Factory and Big, the Tom Hanks film.

They were classics of their kind, but coming from the mouth of this GBH offender it just sounded so unlikely. We both burst out laughing and we were good mates from then on. He wrote me a lovely note when he was released, as did others I shared time with inside.

Wayne was released before me and he's now a chef.

After he left prison, Wayne wrote: "You have become a good

friend as well as a top cell mate. It's been great meeting you and sharing the late night laughs and deep talks.

'Keep your head up bro and be with your family as prison is no place for some-one like you'.

I got on great with Gary, Pete, Fletch and Ash, the other cleaners on my wing. We had our nicknames, Wayne was 'Smokey', Ash was 'Jonny Vegas', Pete was 'Bert' and I was 'Superstar'.

Wayne was replaced as my cellmate by Dwayne, a 50-year old white guy who was inside because he'd found his partner in bed with another man and hurt them both.

His kids were in the house at the time so, understandably, he lost his head and was in Woodhill because of that.

Dwayne was in tears when he explained to me what had happened. It was one of many sad stories I heard when I was in prison.

As you'd expect, prison life is a drudge. We'd be woken at 7am and we'd be doing our chores by 8. We cleaners gave out breakfast to the prisoners – cereal packs rather than porridge - who took them back to the cells to eat.

We did the same before we'd all be let out for a couple of hours of socialising.

Sometimes we were allowed outside for a walk around the yard and I would spend as much free time as possible in the gym. Ironically, I left prison as fit as I'd ever been and I helped a few of the inmates get fit as well.

We were banged up by 7pm for the night, 6pm at weekends. We had a TV with five channels. At times I felt like one of the unemployed with nothing better to do than lounge around and watch Jeremy Kyle.

~ TYPICAL PRISON DAY ~

7am: Bang on the cell door meant time to get up, hand and face wash, teeth cleaning slip into my cleaner's uniform.

7.30am-9.30am: Complete my cleaning jobs, serve breakfast to the other inmates. Take my breakfast to my cell.

9.30am-10.30am: Social time. Hang around the pool room,

communal room for chat, games etc.

10.30am-noon: Locked up again.

Noon-1pm: Out to clean the cells ready for new arrivals.

1pm-3pm: Locked up again.

3pm-4pm: Out for exercise so off to the gym or a walk around the outside compound.

4pm-5pm: Locked up again.

5pm-6pm: Dinner.

6pm-7pm: Socialising in pool room, communal room.

7pm-7am: Locked up. Lights are allowed to be kept on in the cell all night. TV is available, but only five channels.

I was better off inside than some though. At least I had a shower rather than a pokey wash basin.

I was also a worker and I was a trusted worker, so I was often let outside to write the words for this book.

I could spend extra time in the gym if I wanted to as well. I came out in better shape than I went in and I helped other prisoners, particularly a murderer called Martin, get fitter as well.

I wrote every night. It was just me on my own and my thoughts down on the paper in front of me. I found it quite therapeutic. I wanted these words to help people when I came out.

I would re-read the cards and letters I received from my loved ones over and over again, the love I was shown helped me get through the longest two months of my life.

I had pictures of my kids all over the walls of my cell. I had e-mails from Sofia saying she was crying herself to sleep so it wasn't just me suffering, something I had to bear in mind at all times.

Whitney Houston helped me through the worst of it as well. I'd sing her song 'I didn't know my own strength' over and over.

They were lyrics that suited my situation. Whitney was having a lot of issues herself at the time and that and her song just resonated with me.

CHAPTER 8

'ORGANISED KAOS'

It didn't take long for Woodhill to confirm that prison can be a violent place.

I was on the phone to my mum one day when an inmate came tearing past me. There was blood pouring out of his eye and no wonder as he had a pen sticking out of the socket.

No-one batted an eyelid (certainly the injured guy didn't!) except me. If this was the norm, I thought fuck me I can't survive in here, but I was lucky. I was protected.

There were a lot of Muslims inside. They tended to stick together like brothers. The most well-known one who I was aware of was known as Kaos (his real name was the rather less threatening Marcus).

I'd heard of Kaos. He was from Battersea and the word was he was renowned for torture and murder. In fact, he was inside for murder. He knew Harvey as he was also originally from Battersea and more importantly he knew I was a mate of Harvey – that made me safe, although not everyone realised it for a while.

Kaos ruled by fear and reputation. The stories of what he did to the stupid people who dared to cross him were frightening. I'm glad he was on my side.

The prisoners used to play five-a-side football matches in the gym. Obviously I was expected to play, even though only a few knew about the standard I'd played at, so we'd pick sides (I'd make sure Kaos was on mine) and I'd just goal-hang and score from every opportunity that came my way.

I was the Gary Lineker of Woodhill.

In one match I must have scored five in five minutes which riled a big 17-stone Nigerian geezer.

He started mouthing off about breaking some legs. He meant mine.

I confronted him (me being me, I stood up for myself at all times, but I don't know why, as there were some mean fuckers in there) and he wanted to fight me, but we were separated and pledged to meet each other in the changing room afterwards.

We did get close at one point. We were face to face and I took the opportunity to size him up. He was big, but I knew he was bound to be slow. I'd already spotted where I'd throw my punches. My tactics in boxing terms would be to stick and move but before I got a chance to start on him the screws stopped us.

I was in the changing area later as arranged but there was no sign of the Nigerian. That suited me, I'd made my point and he obviously thought better of it. I was quite cocky inside as the Nigerian was a lot bigger than me and I believed I'd made him back off.

But in the gym later a couple of the Muslim brothers beckoned me over. My initial reaction was 'oh shit, what I have I done now? Who have I upset?'

One of the Muslims whispered in my ear: 'Your problem has been sorted. You won't be bothered by the Nigerian anymore.'

The next time I came across the Nigerian, he put his head down and looked at the floor. I had no idea what he'd been threatened with, but it was enough to scare him shitless.

I was a bit disappointed he hadn't been scared off by me, but it was reassuring to have the hardest men in jail on my side.

I had grown a little goatee beard while I was inside so maybe the brothers thought I was a real muslim!

Fights broke out routinely and there were plenty of available weapons. There was a pool table in the communal room so there were cues and balls to smack people about with.

Usually the arguments flared over trivial shit like food portions. One guy was so scared for his life he climbed over some first floor railings and tried to jump before a few of us managed to haul him back in.

It was easy to sharpen objects up in prison which added to the threat of violence.

I even suffered an attack when I was hoovering. Some shifty looking newcomer was prowling about the room giving me the eye.

I ignored him and carried on with my chores. Then I felt a whack in my back. He'd punched me and he was sniggering. Clearly he wasn't all there mentally and they tend to be the more dangerous prisoners.

'Back off'... I warned him. I wasn't really in the mood for a fight that day, but prisoners had started emerging from their cells as they'd heard the commotion. I was on the ground floor, while the in-mates peered down hoping for action.

I picked up the hoover again, but then he punched me again. Now the adrenaline was pumping and I had a crowd to impress.

This pillock just smirked at me and then he came for me again. I slipped his punch to the left and hit him with a overhand left that staggered him.

He made the mistake of getting up and charging again, so I dropped to my right and unleashed a right uppercut into his ribcage and flattened him. He was, by now, gasping for air but I still backed him off even further with a serious left hand.

The crowd loved it. I'd delivered another statement about not messing with me.

I had a few scraps, but never got in trouble with the screws about it. Indeed, they congratulated me on the way I broke up certain situations like when my room-mate Wayne was threatened by a short, black guy from South London.

The cleaners were always getting asked by inmates to sneak stuff out of the kitchens and offices, but some days you just couldn't be arsed.

Wayne, who could be a bit of a loose cannon, adopted that attitude one day, but he told the wrong man to go fuck himself.

Shorty told me to sort my boy out or he'd sort him out himself, but I was becoming something of a mediator inside and, luckily for Wayne, I calmed the situation down.

The screws were impressed as well and my stock had now risen further inside. These were still challenging times for me but I was keeping busy and doing some good which certainly helped me cope mentally.

You always had to be on your toes inside. Periods of calm were often followed by tense encounters between dangerous men, the sort you'd cross the road to avoid on the outside.

The screws were generally okay with me although I had to step in on one occasion and sort one out.

He was forever dissing me. He was never happy with what I was doing or how I did it.

He was like the worst kind of teacher. He was bossy, power-crazed, obnoxious. He used to call me 'McKenzie' using an annoying tone, unlike the other screws. He was a bit power crazed and he'd speak to me like I was a bit of dirt on his shoe.

I stormed into his office one day. Told him I was sick of his attitude, it was all bullshit and if he wanted to fuck my life up even more then go ahead. I was already in prison and I didn't think it could get much worse than that.

He explained to me that the screws were told to act tough at all times. Some of the people they were guarding would not react positively to kindness. They would abuse it.

The screw was more shocked that I stood up to him. That was my way though and I never had a problem with him after that – in fact I grew to see him as a top lad.

Indeed I found most of the screws okay. We only had one prison officer for each 100 inmates, but there was rarely any trouble.

I'd see the odd bundle when a few screws would pile into a cell, but generally there was a mutual respect between staff and 'guest'. I got on particularly well with two personal trainers based in the gym. They looked after me well when I was keeping fit. I can't remember their names, but they will know who they are!

There was even an ex-professional footballer who worked as a senior prison officer at Woodhill.

Paul Dyson was best known for playing for Coventry in the Football League so we had an obvious bond.

It was Paul who sorted out my tag for me. It wasn't guaranteed that your sentence (in my case three months) would be cut and you would be released under licence with a tag attached to your lower leg, a device that ensured you had to observe a curfew.

You had to behave yourself in there, but Paul was the one who pushed me towards applying for the tag and helped me fill out the request forms.

Mr Crannie was the prison officer who secured me the job of cleaner on the second day of my sentence and that might not sound a big deal, but believe me getting on the cleaning staff was a big perk on the inside.

There was even an officer at Woodhill called Mr King who did card tricks and a Mr Bird who was forever finding me phone credit.

I had some fascinating and deep conversations with a Mr Crickmore. He was a bit older than the others, but we talked for hours about the prison system and why it doesn't work.

And then there was Mr Capon, an officer who some of the prisoners thought was a bit of a bully and who certainly did everything by the book.

Mr Capon had a habit of rubbing everyone up the wrong way. I was certainly a bit more wary of him than the others and we almost had a massive falling out on one of the occasions when I was having a rough day.

It was my daughter Talia's first birthday and I was inside so naturally I wasn't in the best of moods. Mr Capon realised I wasn't happy, but, obviously, he didn't know why.

When I was in a bad mood, everyone knew about it and everyone realised it was best to steer clear of me.

Instead Mr Capon approached me and warned me he would report me if my attitude didn't improve. Basically going on report would mean the loss of a few privileges, but I just snapped and told him to do what he had to do and I'd live with the consequences.

The atmosphere was immediately hostile, but he backed off and to be fair to him when the time came for my release Mr Capon came to me and praised me for my conduct while I was inside.

He said I could leave prison with my head held high and that was a great boost for me because he didn't have to say that.

All of these men were of great help to me and so were the women prison officers, although God only knows how they did that job.

Miss Beer and Miss Dennison were the two on my ward. They were sweet girls, but they were also as tough as the men.

I admired them for the way they dealt with the inevitable 'jokes' and abuse that headed their way.

Miss Beer was a real joker and Miss Dennison was always passing the time of day with me. She had to back off when she realised I was a bit of a charmer as it wasn't the done thing to get too close to the prisoners.

~BROKEN SYSTEM~

Prison horrified me. It's a system that clearly doesn't work.

The kids treat it like a social club. Lads of 19, 20 and 21 would habitually re-offend. They found it easier to be inside with their mates then to be on the outside where they would have responsibilities towards paying bills and feeding themselves.

They get three meals a day in prison for a start. Their laundry would be done for them.

These lads would be freed, but you just knew that many of them would be back inside within weeks. Maybe not at this prison, but the system would lock them up again somehow.

As far as I could see, there was no attempt at rehabilitation for these lads. They were caught in a vicious circle and it used to horrify me.

I once saw a 73 year-old come in to this category A prison for not paying his TV licence. It just bewildered me that there were judges and prosecutors out there who thought sending a frail man of that age inside was the right thing to do and for such a trivial offence.

But worst of all I saw people who were clearly unwell. They were drug addicts who would have been better off getting de-toxed in hospital, rather than mixing with similar types in an environment that hardly discouraged the use of illegal substances.

There were de-tox sessions inside. I knew this as I often had to wait around to serve food to the prisoners who went along to them. But when I saw them, they'd still be out of their heads.

It was obvious to me what the problem was. These de-tox sessions clearly didn't work as they could still buy drugs inside!

It wasn't difficult. Even if the prisoners had no money on the inside, they could get their friends on the outside to pay into the suppliers' bank accounts.

There was random drug testing inside, but I doubt it made any difference. I was tested myself twice, but obviously I passed!

Drugs were readily available to anyone who wanted them and everyone knew from where and from whom. All sorts of smuggling techniques were used to defeat the screws. I saw a guy take a balloon out of his arse on one occasion.

If the courts thought that sending drug addicts to prison would cause some effective 'cold turkey' they were sadly misguided. I didn't get involved, but I would guess it was easier to buy drugs in prison than on the outside.

There was a prison chaplain and I went to see him once, but he did nothing for me. There were too many prisoners there who weren't taking the opportunity seriously enough.

It was just another meeting for them, another chance to have a laugh and a joke with their mates outside of their cells.

Maybe getting a bit of faith and direction in their lives would have helped some of them, but they just weren't interested.

One or two took it seriously. A couple of older guys were trying to keep their faith, but they would get so badly mistreated and bullied by the younger kids I felt really sorry for them.

The chaplain seemed to be a good man, but I didn't go back. I was pretty much on my own in there with just my own dreams to keep me going.

However, I did start offering my own counselling service. I didn't actually have much of a choice as youngsters would regularly come to me for advice on dealing with their issues.

It didn't seem to matter to them that all I'd done was play professional football.

A man convicted of murder once asked me how he was supposed to cope with a 13 year sentence. He'd only completed two years at the time.

'Mate' I said 'I've been here two weeks and there's no way I'll be coming back. Isn't being stuck in here enough of a deterrent?'

We started chatting properly and he explained that just as I had been a professional footballer all my life, he had been a professional criminal. To him crime was a job and he said he couldn't give it up any easier than I could give up football.

It was sad but true.

I don't know how he expected me to help, but I did my best and it made me feel good about myself. The younger ones reckoned it must be cool to be a professional footballer and loved chatting to me.

I rammed it into them that there are always choices, that most of them were young enough to turn their lives around, that they had to dump the hangers-on (I ditched many when I left Woodhill), be more careful about who they mixed with and don't be so easily influenced.

There were a lot of weak men in there. Big lads who had robbed banks or had been sent to prison for beating people up would come into my cell and cry their eyes out about missing their kids.

They only knew a life of crime. To them being a criminal was all they knew, but I had a dream list in my head of things away from football that I wanted to achieve success in, most notably my music (irritatingly my debut single had been released while I was in prison).

I advised some of those who came to see me to make their own list of dreams, but to be honest most were too deep into the routine of offend, prison, offend, prison – it was a cycle they couldn't break.

I was determined that every time I failed I would get stronger. I tried to drum that sort of message into drug users, violent men and murderers and I suspect that was the only advice they ever received while prisoners of the system.

The system didn't beat me though. The CPS, the higher ranking police officers in Northampton and Judge Bray had all tried to break me with their actions so it was a good job I had a strong chin.

I didn't need to be in prison. One night in a cell in a police station in Northampton had been enough to convince me to never, ever mess with the law again.

I felt like I was used as an example, as a warning to other well known people that no-one is above the law.

I was stuck inside to make others feel good and it was just so unnecessary. I held my hands up and told the truth from the minute I was first questioned and yet here I was - a depressed, suicidal man don't forget - being invited to sink deeper into my personal torment.

They didn't break me though. They pushed me down to the bottom and they tested my character, but I got back up and I emerged stronger.

I no longer have any respect for the system. In my opinion there are a few policemen bend the law and I knew they did to me. It's been proved they did regarding Hillsborough.

They will clearly do anything to cover their own backs even if it means fucking up other people's lives.

I'd been locked up for a little crime and now my chance of getting a job on the outside was going to be difficult purely because someone had put a stain on my record that I didn't deserve.

The work I did with the inmates was good practice for me though. It made me even more determined to help footballers in trouble when I was freed.

When I was preparing to leave, there was no counselling about what to do back on the outside. The big day of my release came and the wardens and inmates queued up to shake my hand and to repeat their belief that I'd been stitched up good and proper.

I put my suit back on and that felt cool, like I was a real human being again. I picked up my bag, the main door was opened and out I marched.

I was actually in shock. This should have been one of the happiest days of my life, but not only did I not have a clue what the future held, I was still raging about the sheer injustice of my situation.

Obviously, it was going to be great to see Sofia and the kids again, but I had a criminal record so would I even be able to get a job?

Sofia met me at the prison gates and it was an emotional moment. We cried, we hugged and the kids were thrilled dad had returned from his music trip.

I had served three months, but I had to wear a tag for a fourth month. I had to be at home between the hours of 7pm and 7am.

I played a charity football match in Sheffield once and my tag broke which forced some miserable woman to come out and visit me.

Luckily, you get one life before they throw the book at you. I was back at home on time every day after that, I wasn't taking any risks.

Once on the outside, I immediately locked certain people out of my life. People I had trusted and loved dumped me when I was inside and I wasn't prepared to forget about that.

I cut off a lot of people when I was released. When something bad like going to prison happens, you find out who your true friends are, like Dubes, like Jason Lee and Darren Byfield, my cousin

Damien and our mate Daniel, Bruce Dyer, Harvey and Spoony,
They stayed in touch, but not getting a single letter or message
from some members of my big family, that hurt me.

But I was surely through the worst now though. I felt that, with
some huge help from my closest friends and family, I had made
a breakthrough which would help me get through the rest of my
life.

If I could survive three months in prison I could survive anything.
Physically, I was free from prison, but more importantly, my
mind had also been freed of dangerously negative thoughts.

I was happy inside my head and looking forward to the rest of
my life.

CHAPTER 9

'PRINCE OF THE PALACE'

Most of the younger prisoners I met on the inside were fascinated by the life of a professional footballer. Many in Woodhill had seen me play for Crystal Palace and we spent many hours recalling some of my favourite moments.

I loved talking about my debut as a professional for Palace which remains one of the greatest days I ever experienced in football.....

.....Dean Gordon was in possession on the left. He played a one-two with Bruce Dyer, and crossed the ball into the six yard box.

I met the ball on the volley with my left foot and the ball whistled into the net. The Selhurst Park crowd went mad and no wonder.

A 17 year-old local boy had scored on his first-team debut for Crystal Palace. It was only Southend and it was only the League Cup, but it was a massive deal for me.

Of all people, chairman Ron Noades- a man I had a lot of time for as he looked after me well- had told me I was playing.

My grandad Fred had been moaning about me not getting picked for a youth team match and Ron had to calm him down by telling him why.

Very calmly, Ron said it was because I was playing for the first team as Dougie Freedman was cup-tied.

It was the first I'd heard of it! Manager Steve Coppell hadn't mentioned it and nor had the youth team coaches.

But it was true and I was in the dressing room before the match with the likes of Chris Coleman, Gareth Southgate, who was a central midfielder in those days, and Ray Houghton.

The Palace team was: Nigel Martyn, Jamie Vincent, Dean Gordon, Chris Coleman, Richard Shaw, Andy Roberts, Ray Houghton, Gareth Southgate, Darren Pitcher, Bruce Dyer, Leon McKenzie.

Strangely, I felt at home. I was confident I would play well and I just knew I would score, especially as half of South London had turned up to watch a local boy in action.

I had a swagger about me in those days, but I worked hard in every game, chasing lost causes and generally making a nuisance of myself.

The ground seemed to erupt when I opened the scoring (a goal you can still find onYouTube). We won 2-0 and I had my first taste of media attention. I enjoyed this sort more than some of my other confrontations with the press later in life.

The day after the game, Noades and Coppell called me in. They wanted me to sign a pro deal. I was offered £250 a week and a £10,000 signing on fee. I had no agent, but I had my dad and grandad in the room with me, and I signed straight away with no hassling or negotiation as I just wanted to play professionally. The £10,000 was a huge amount of money, but I spent it on trainers, clothes and stuff like any teenager would. It didn't last long.

But the pro contract was worth twice as much to me. It was the realisation of a dream. I could call myself a pro footballer and that had its perks.

Signing that first professional contract was one of the best days of my life. My dad's determination to be a success in his sport had rubbed off on me. I had given everything to become a pro, put my heart and soul into it, and I had earned everything I had achieved.

I remember my dad opening the door to me when I came home after my debut, smiling and embracing me in one of his powerful bear hugs.

It was a beautiful feeling that I could make members of my loving family so proud of me

I had seen dad going out for runs at 4am and come back hours later to do sit-ups. He told me that hard work would bring rewards and he was right, not that I was ready for all of it.

~ A DAD AT 18 ~

"You fucking idiot, you've ruined your career!" They are not the words an 18-year-old who'd just signed his first professional contract would want to hear.

They came from the mouth of Palace youth team boss Brian Sparrow and he'd been provoked by me telling him that I was to become a dad.

I'd moved in with my girlfriend Vanessa into her place at Herne Hill. She was 24 (although I didn't know that at the time, she'd told me she was 21) and I was 17. It wasn't the usual move for a young footballer, but I was happy enough.

Sparrow wasn't happy at all though and he ranted and raved for ages. I'm sure he was trying to knock the star player about a bit just to prove who was the boss, but eventually I burst into tears and roared 'fuck off, fuck off' at him."

Coppell's room was next door and he came rushing in, grabbed me and hustled me into his office.

Coppell was a great bloke and a real inspiration for me. He was so calm in just about every situation and I just explained my personal situation to him and he asked me just one question.

"Leon, are you happy?" he said. I thought I was, told him so, and that was that. Nothing else mattered. He offered a secure little smile and I just knew I was going to love working for this man.

Coppell was very influential in my football career. He was a quiet man, but he was intelligent. He barely wasted a word and when he did speak the whole first-team squad, which included some pretty big names in those days, listened because he had a way of getting his point across so everyone in the room understood what he wanted.

He was the perfect manager for a youngster like me trying to break into the first team. We had one-on-one sessions together at our training ground in Mitcham because he could see my hunger and he wanted that in his team.

Coppell used to tell me that I reminded him of Ian Wright and Norman Whiteside. Wright was also a player with great desire as well as natural ability, while Whiteside broke into the Manchester United team at 17 and Coppell felt I could do the same at Palace.

My earliest memory of Coppell the manager was watching him, when I was a youngster, running down the touchline like one of the brothers when Palace scored the winning goal in the FA Cup semi-final against Liverpool!

That was so out of character as he was normally the epitome of cool.

~ WEMBLEY WIN AND THE PREMIER LEAGUE ~

Not that Coppell played me much in my first full season as a pro (1996-97). I was on the bench for three-quarters of the season.

It had been the same after my debut the previous season. I made a dozen or so appearances after that Southend match, but all of them as a substitute.

I was keen for my career to take off but Coppell kept stressing the need for patience. He had Bruce Dyer and Freedman as his first choice strikers in those days and they were both quality performers.

We didn't start the season well, but we soon hit our stride. I remember one glorious spell when we won 6-1 at Reading and beat Southend 6-1 at home as well as beating Manchester City 3-1 at Selhurst Park.

I wasn't even getting on the substitutes' bench then, but I could hardly complain as the team kept winning. I was doing my stuff in the reserves and getting the odd call-up to the first-team.

I did score a couple of goals in successive games towards the end of the season which helped us beat Norwich and Oldham, but I knew my place!

Palace finished in a play-off place and we saw off Wolves quite comfortably over two legs to book a place at Wembley in the final against Sheffield United.

I was put on the substitutes' bench which was great for an 18 year-old and I had my whole family there for the big day.

The final was a tight old match against Sheffield United with few chances. I was told to warm-up as Coppell wanted to send me on for extra time. Some of our players were flagging and Coppell thought my pace and strength could tip the balance.

But then David Hopkins decided he would score a world-class goal into the top corner of United's net in the last minute of normal time to win the game.

I was delighted of course – I'd be a Premier League player as a teenager for a start –but I was a little frustrated as well because I just knew I would have scored if I'd got on the pitch.

That's how confident I was in my ability. Playing at Wembley didn't worry me, it excited me.

I was one of the lesser youth players when I first joined Palace and within two years I was the star man with more technical skill and raw ability than anyone – I felt I'd made a massive statement. I was still eligible to play for the youths after I signed my first professional contract. I scored plenty of goals for them and the reserve team.

I'd been tagged as the next Ian Wright (a Palace legend) and I wanted the first-team staff to believe in me. I was still learning of course, but I was impatient as I knew I was capable of much more improvement.

Coppell was always encouraging though. He would watch me kick balls at walls so I could practice my control and technique. He knew I was putting the hours in.

~ WILKINS AND KEEGAN ~

Coppell sent me on loan to Fulham early in my days as a professional. He wanted me to get some experience.

Ray Wilkins was managing Fulham at the time. He'd seen me play for Palace and he knew what I was capable of.

I came on as a substitute in a couple of games and then I made my full debut for Fulham against Bournemouth and I was rubbish. Every ball bounced off me, every pass went astray and I never looked like scoring.

It was one of those days that even the top players have from time to time. I was utterly hopeless, it was one of the worst performances of my life.

Naturally, Wilkins wasn't impressed and he wanted me to play in a reserve game a few days later. I refused. I turned this legend of the game down without a second thought.

I could have stayed at Palace and played reserve team football to a higher standard than Fulham were offering me.

I didn't see the logic in going somewhere on loan and playing in their reserves. Fulham were in the third division at the time.

I told Wilkins what I thought so he sent me back to Palace that day. He didn't think much to my attitude.

Kevin Keegan had arrived at Fulham by then (he was chief operating officer under Wilkins) and he pulled me to one side.

Keegan said I was going to be a top-class striker one day if I kept progressing at the same rate, but he also warned me to never, ever refuse to play again, no matter how strongly I felt about things.

He liked the fact that I was single-minded and that I was prepared to stand up for what I believed in, but he said pissing powerful people off was not conducive to a long career like his.

It was sound advice. Keegan gave me his number and we kept in touch for a bit. He was a great player and a great bloke.

Keegan was also a great coach. I loved the drills he used to put on for the strikers. He was down to earth and hard to dislike because of his sheer enthusiasm.

There was no lasting damage to my relationship with Wilkins either. We bumped into each other a while later and there were clearly no hard feelings between us. I apologised to Ray as it was wrong at that time of my career to behave as I did towards someone like him. I put it down to frustration and he accepted my explanation and he seemed to gain respect for me because I'd taken the trouble to apologise.

Wilkins explained to me that he was stressed at the time. Fulham was politically a difficult place to work as Keegan and Mohammed Al Fayed were pulling the strings and demanding instant success. Coppell was a bit concerned that I'd come back early from the loan, but as usual he supported me when I told him exactly what happened.

I actually told him that I missed him which made him laugh. He said that sort of behaviour didn't sound like the Leon he knew so we just put it to one side and got on with things at Palace.

Anyway, at just 18 years old I was in a good place professionally with a winner's medal from Wembley in my hand and the status of Premier League footballer. Dad was so proud of me.

I made four appearances as a sub that season, three of them in the Premier League, and that was fair enough as I was so far out of my depth it was frightening.

I came on in an FA Cup replay against Arsenal and they had Martin Keown, Lee Dixon, Tony Adams and Matthew Upson at the back, David Platt and Patrick Vieira in midfield and Nicolas Anelka and Dennis Bergkamp up front.

Marc Overmars came on as a substitute and I couldn't believe I was mixing it with these players at my age. We only lost that game 2-1 as well despite playing for most of it with 10 men after Dean Gordon was sent off.

I didn't manage a goal in those rare Premier League appearances and we were relegated.

We had actually started the season okay and won our first two away games at Everton and Leeds. We also won at Spurs, but we would go on long losing runs, particularly towards the end of the season when we lost 13 out of 15 to send us to the bottom of the league.

The season really passed me by. Coppell quit towards the end of it and was replaced by Attilio Lombardo, but the following season we were to be coached by Terry Venables.

The first thing Venables did to me was to send me on loan to Peterborough and that worked well for me. I scored twice on my debut at Cardiff and became an instant hero with their fans.

It was a lovely little time which got me scoring goals and gave me confidence. Unfortunately, after a handful of games I picked up an injury and had to go back.

Venables was different class though. He understood players and he understood the game. We didn't have the greatest results under him, but the lads loved his methods and we were very disappointed that we didn't do better for a popular bloke.

Venables was a clever businessman as well as a decent coach. He realised I'd done well at Peterborough and that other clubs would have noticed so the first thing he did when I came back to Palace was to offer me a new contract.

This would give me decent bargaining power if I ended up talking to a new club. He didn't have to do it, but he did.

I was now on £1200 per week, but ended back on loan at Peterborough as soon as my injury cleared up.

By the time I got back to Palace, I was disappointed to find that Venables had gone, but I was thrilled that Coppell had come back. Venables had been re-appointed Palace boss by a new chairman Mark Goldberg who had promised his new manager the earth.

The players had heard it all before in the world of football. We christened Goldberg 'The Penguin', but we had to respect his vision and ambition for the club.

He delivered Venables which was a coup as he wouldn't have worked for peanuts, but the promise of new players (another thing Venables would have demanded when he returned) didn't materialise and it was soon obvious that the club were still struggling financially.

Above: Celebrating my 100th career goal after being out from a ruptured thigh, it was a great feeling

Image [PA]

Right:My Dad and I winning the British title for a 3rd time beating Lloyd Christie in 1989

Image Michael Fresco / Evening Standard / Solo Syndication

Above: Me when I was 4 Years Old

Left:My Grandad Fred, I miss him, My number 1 fan

Right: Our wedding day to my Queen B! Sofia McKenzie

Above: My four beautiful babies: Kasey, Mariya, Naima and Talia

Right:Arriving at court, keeping it together
Picture courtesy of Northampton Chronicle & Echo/Sharon Lucey

Above: Celebrating a goal for Posh for my beautiful sister Tracey who passed away Image Peterborough ET

Above: My Princess, Champ and Sweetpea

Above: Me and my amazing Mummy at Naima's christening

Above: Me and my sister Rebecca at Headcorn Road home

Above: Signed YTS for Crystal Palace with my Dad, Grandad Fred and youth team coach Peter Nicolas

Above: Me and Hucks having a moment after my goal, Dream Team

Image [PA]

Left: My Sister Tracey I love and miss her loads I always see your smile

Below Left: Me and Queen B in Las Vegas

Below Right: My MOTM gift on my debut, overwhelmed at 17 years old

Above: Scoring another goal for Posh, 1 of many, good times
Image Peterborough ET

Above: Me and Talia, the baby of the family, but don't let her fool you. She can fight. Haha!

It wasn't the greatest surprise when the club fell into administration. Coppell kept Palace going through some horrible times and he deserved the greatest of respect for that.

For about three months, we weren't getting paid and that was a massive problem for me as I wasn't on the best money and I was the sole financial provider in my household.

Coppell was brilliant though. He'd get me in his office and make me want to play for him for nothing.

He'd tell me to think how good it would make me look to the fans and the outside world that I was happy to roll my sleeves up and fight for a club even though I wasn't getting paid.

Coppell was such an intelligent man. I'm sure he was saying those things to all the players and the result was a string of committed displays, especially from the younger players who were hit the hardest by the money issues as we had no savings.

It was masterful man management and Palace should be eternally grateful for the work Coppell did when times were really hard.

I started a few games, but then I'd be a substitute for a few more. I was just happy to help Coppell and the club though.

As a club, we were still a bit down after our relegation, but in the circumstances we did well to limp to a 14th place finish.

~ RACISM AND FIGHT CLUBS ~

"Leon you black bastard, hold the fucking ball up."

The training session stopped. There was a stunned silence, no-one could believe what they'd heard.

The words came from another player we had at Palace. It might have been normal language for him, but I wasn't having it.

I sprinted from the halfway line and pulled up just short of this idiot. I didn't say a word, but I dropped him with one punch.

He got up so I dropped him again. "Stay down," I screamed. He did. All the other lads left him there, but congratulated me.

I never really experienced racism from opponents or from football supporters, but I did from a supposed team-mate.

He never did understand why I got so upset. That's how he used to speak all the time apparently.

The only other time I experienced racism in football was many years later when I went to Greece for the summer to have a trial with Kerkyra FC.

I played in one game when every time I touched the ball I would hear monkey chants. It was accepted as normal out there, so much so that I wouldn't have been surprised if the managers had joined in.

It's very sad that such blatant racism exists in many places all over the world. Some people use the word 'nigger' as often as they say 'hello'. They weren't born racist, they have it instilled in them from an early age.

They are ignorant and shallow. I am proud of the colour of my skin from a white mum and a black dad. I have the best of both cultures in me.

Anyway, He hardly played for Palace. Mainly because he was no good, rather than any racism hangover, but he was pretty much shunned by the rest of the squad after the incident with me and it was no surprise when he left the club soon afterwards.

I knew he was shocked by my onslaught, but I can't remember him ever apologising for what he said.

I already had a bit of a reputation as someone who could look after myself. I was surprised, especially as they knew my boxing background, why anyone would take me on physically.

Sometimes you just had to fight, even with team-mates. You had to stand up for yourself, for what you believed in.

I was also happy to fight on behalf of my friends. I had a few good pals at Palace like Clinton Morrison, Sagi Burton and Bobby Bowry.

Morrison was what you'd call a character. You'd either love him or hate him. I've felt both for him, but he's still my mate now and we abuse and banter with each other on Twitter.

I understood Clinton, but not everyone did. He was a real showboater and he found it easy to rub people up the wrong way.

His mum, Angela, told me once to slap him if he ever gave me any trouble!

Clinton could over-step the mark with some of his comments. I had to pull him to one side and warn him off a few times.

During one training jog, Clinton and a young player called Sam Noonan, a youth team lad who never won a pro contract, started on one another and it was soon getting heated with more than a hint of violence.

I managed to get between them and for some reason, some silly reason which he probably regrets to this day, Sam started on me. It was the worst mistake of his life.

He squared up to me. I adopted my boxing stance and whack I smacked him. He came again so I had to smack him twice more.

Sam was a brave little fucker I'll give him that, but the rest of the lads were laughing at him as he was totally over-matched. Strange thing was he apologised to me the next day for starting the trouble and he told the lads there was nothing he could do in the fight as I was far too fast for him.

It was also strange that for all the punch-ups I had in my career I never once got fined by my club.

The Palace lads liked a night out and it didn't always end well. One Christmas a certain player was smashed and for some reason he decided to lash out at another, but he had a glass in his hand when he did it.

The glass shattered in this player's face and there was blood everywhere. I was still a kid and couldn't believe what was happening as the lad got led away to have some stitches inserted in an ugly wound.

The drunk player was embarrassed by what he did and apologised to everyone the next morning. He was a good lad who was a lot older than me and it was totally out of character, but some things we do are beyond explanation, especially after a few drinks.

The injured lad took it well though. He knew it was just high jinks and that he hadn't meant to glass him.

Andy Preece also got a smack when we were in a nightclub once, but his pain proved a lot funnier to the rest of us.

Southgate, Richard Shaw, Chris Coleman, Simon Rodger, Bobby Bowry and me and a few others were out in the Blue Orchid club in Croydon.

We were drinking, we were laughing, we were chatting up girls, but what we didn't know was that some of the players' wives and girlfriends were upstairs in the club and were spying on us.

They'd found out where we were going and followed us in so they could keep an eye us. They must have heard about some of the things we got up to.

Anyway all of a sudden, out of nowhere, a woman appeared right behind Preece and slapped him in the back of his head and in his face. We were stunned until we realised it was his wife.

We were all targets for women because we were footballers and had a bit of cash. We liked a drink, but there wasn't a drinking culture as such.

I actually spent most of my afternoons, once training had finished food shopping, baby-sitting and other parental stuff. I was happy doing that.

I didn't even go out that much at weekends and if I did Vanessa didn't like it.

When I became a bit more mature, I used to hang out with Richard Rufus, Shaun Newton and Bruce Dyer. Bruce was a DJ back in the day and we did get up to mischief, but nothing too serious.

We had plenty of fun during the close season and girls were always throwing themselves at us and it was hard to refuse. For me it was anyway.

We had characters at Palace. Chris Armstrong, a top player at Palace who went on to play for Spurs, was done for smoking marijuana once, but dealt with the inevitable stick from the lads by walking around pretending to smoke the stuff all the time.

After Armstrong was caught our partying was toned down. A footballer failing a drugs test was unusual in those days and everyone automatically became a lot more careful.

Towards the end of my time at Palace, Neil Ruddock joined us.

What a laugh he was. I hit it off with him straight away. He called me Rimmer because of my use of the racquet frame when we used to play tennis together.

One pre-season, we were running. It was hard, it was hot and Razor didn't fancy it. He did one lap, stopped and lay down on the grass.

Our manager was Alan Smith at the time (I thought he was an oddball and I didn't like him) and his attempts to persuade Razor to get up were embarrassing and funny.

Razor wasn't interested, said he wasn't fucking running anymore and just got up and left. That was my first experience of player-power as Smith had no control over him.

~ STARS IN HIS EYES ~

There were some high class players at Palace when I broke into the senior squad.

Ray Houghton was one. He was at the back-end of his career and he moaned more often and for longer than any other player I've ever played with (only Michael Doyle at Coventry came close and he won't mind me saying that as he's my mate today).

Every time he misplaced a pass, it would be the striker's fault for moving too soon or too late, or you'd made the wrong run.

Nine times out of 10, he was probably right though. I was only a teenager so I had to agree with everything a player who had achieved pretty much everything in the game had to say.

Ray kept me on my toes. I knew he saw I had great ability and it was his way of trying to help me.

Gareth Southgate was an absolute gentleman. He was club captain at Palace, but he lead by example rather than by shouting. He was a calm man, very placid and used to avoid confrontations. When I played against him for Norwich (he was at Middlesbrough) it gave me a thrill that I could compete with international stars.

He was a generous opponent as well and just a lovely man full stop.

Attilio Lombardo was a funny looking bloke. Small, bald and he had a funny run. He also loved a cigarette and a glass of wine (he was Italian after all), but what a consummate professional he was.

He was still a fantastic player when he was with us. He had so much footballing intelligence and he insisted on sharing his wisdom with the youngsters.

He gave me tips on exercise and generally on anything to do with being a professional on and off the pitch. I didn't dare ask him why he thought it was professional to smoke heavily and to drink bottle after bottle of wine.

Sasa Curcic is one of the craziest men I've ever met. He was a superb player, but only when he could be bothered.

The management at Palace didn't know how to get the best out of him. Curcic used to have blazing, foul-mouthed rows with reserve team coach Steve Kember.

Kember was old school, a hard-working, not particularly talented player, but he was Palace through and through. The exact opposite of Curcic in other words!

Curcic went on the Serbian version of Big Brother when he retired. He won it which didn't surprise anyone who knew him, nor did the fact that he blew all the winnings on strippers and prostitutes.

Curcic went on the show with the memorable line: "I have given up football because I prefer sex. I would rather score in bed than on the pitch."

That was so typical of him.

Ashley Cole came to Palace when he was a kid at Arsenal. He looked up to me then and we still speak now and again.

When Ashley joined us I saw a player who was already special. He stood out as a huge talent even as a kid, but as I was a bit older than him I took it upon myself to tell him to keep working hard in order to fulfil his potential.

It seems weird now that he thanked me for helping him. For me he's still the best left-back in the world.

Ian Wright had left Palace by the time I got there, but he was a great help in my career. He was such a charismatic character, always positive and always there to lift me up when I was down.

It was an honour that he gave me his phone number and told me to call him whenever I wanted. He and John Barnes were my playing heroes when I was growing up.

I would ring him when I wasn't scoring as often as I liked. His advice was invaluable, just speaking to some-one of that character would give me a boost.

My last conversation with Ian came while I was down in the dumps at Charlton.

I was really struggling, but I didn't have the heart to tell Ian that I was suffering from depression and needed help so I sent him a text message to say I was thinking of quitting football.

He rang back, but I missed the call. However Ian had left a really uplifting message saying he didn't want to hear all that negative talk.

He told me I had to believe in myself, that I had always scored goals and that was just a bad patch that all top goal-scorers go through. He was sure I would come good again.

His words really hit home. I knew my heart and body were failing, but thanks to Ian's encouragement and wisdom I decided to give it another shot at Northampton.

I thank Ian for always having the time to talk to me and encourage me. He is a great man as far as I'm concerned.

Other Palace players weren't so well known, but still deserve recognition. Players like Danny Boxall.

He was talented, but injuries stopped him getting to the top. And a liking for KFC didn't help either.

One Friday after training, we sneaked off to get some KFC ahead of an away trip, but we got the time of the coach departure wrong. We ended up getting on the team bus holding KFC in our hands. It wasn't the sort of diet encouraged in professional football and Ray Lewington went mad.

We were the two youngest players in the team at the time and the rest of the squad couldn't believe what we had done.

We got away with it just, mainly because Lewington was a good man who knew we were both dedicated to our profession.

Rob Quinn was another I enjoyed playing with. He is now an Academy coach at Palace and looks after my cousin Ellis (Uncle Duke's son) who had ambitions of reaching the first team, He certainly couldn't be starting out at a better club.

CHAPTER 10

'GOD HELP ME'

Iloved Crystal Palace. I was the local boy made good. I could see myself playing for the club for a long time. I certainly didn't believe that my new-found religious convictions would lead to me leaving.

I was 20 when I became a born-again Christian. I found God at a time when I needed him. I was beginning to question my lifestyle. A good friend, Zephaniah, introduced me to a church in Norbury and initially I found peace there. I was content.

It was inspiring to have a relationship with God and to have faith that God would look after me and put certain beneficial things into my life.

But the church elders bounced me into getting married when I was too young. I was living with Vanessa when I joined the church, but the elders wanted me to be a role model and that meant a wedding rather than living in sin.

The church also had some wrong 'uns in positions of responsibility – false prophets the bible would call them - and I was appalled when I heard stories about money going missing and I was disgusted when they humiliated a friend of mine and his girlfriend.

Their sin had been for her to fall pregnant when they weren't married. Their punishment was to stand up in front of the entire congregation and make grovelling apologies.

They were mocked mercilessly and I didn't like it. I lost my own way soon afterwards and I'm still trying to find a way back to God.

~ CATCHING THE EYE ~

I had joined Palace after leaving school at 15. I'd made a few people sit up and notice me when I played in a five-a-side tournament at Chipstead FC, one of the clubs I played for as a youngster.

The Chipstead manager was Alan Brett who was a massive help in my development as a footballer.

I owned Chipstead that day. I played up front on my own, banged in goal after goal and everyone was asking who I was.

Throughout that particular season, I was scoring in every game I played in every competition and the attention I was getting was overwhelming.

I was raw, but I was tough and I had a knack for goal-scoring. Paul Nicholas was the Palace Youth Team manager back then and his son was at my school and told me his dad was aware of me and that I should ring him.

Palace had been watching me for a while and so I found out later had Fulham. I'm surprised I hadn't spotted these scouts as there weren't exactly many people watching us play!

When I left school, I wrote to every club in the country asking for a trial, but only six replied and none were interested. I was heart-broken as I felt I just needed an opportunity to prove that I could make it.

I finally plucked up the courage to ring Nicholas. I pleaded with him to give this local boy a chance. If I failed at least I would have tried and not making it would have been down to me.

He could tell I was desperate, but he also realised that I was hungry and determined. He eventually gave in and invited me down to train with the Palace youth team – in no time I realised how far behind the others I was in terms of technique, fitness and general ability.

It was an eye-opener, but I always gave everything a go. This time everything was on the line and it was a different ball game because I was miles behind the others.

I could score goals in the sessions, but if you lost control of the ball even for a split second, as I often did, it would be whipped off your toes.

I was used to being the best player on the pitch and now I was among the worst. Most of the youth team lads were older and bigger than me of course which still made a difference at that age, but I had the biggest heart and my motivation was as high as everyone else's.

Nicholas was an outstanding coach and that was just what I needed to catch up with the others. I was a quick, little striker whose only real asset was scoring, but he taught me how to hold the ball up, what runs to make and other bits to get me up to the level of the others.

My initial trial was supposed to be a fortnight, but six months on I was still turning up every day and not getting paid. Nicholas would come to me at the end of every week and tell me I was doing well, but that I needed to do even better.

If he was testing my resolve, I must have passed. Of course, I was irritated that it was taking them so long to make a decision, but the longer I waited the more determined I became.

I realise now that Nicholas and his staff must have seen some potential because they spent an awful lot of time with me bringing me up to scratch and I will always be grateful for their efforts.

Finally, after another long session, Nicholas called me into his office and I assumed he was just going to repeat what he'd said for the previous six months and tell me to keep plugging away and to keep improving.

I would have agreed of course, but this time Steve Coppell, the Palace first-team manager, was in the room.

Coppell told me that he and the youth team staff had been so impressed with my willingness to graft and put the hours in, in order to improve and make the grade, they were now offering me a two-year apprenticeship.

I was like 'wow' I've made it. All the hours, days and weeks spent fighting, just for the slightest chance of making it in professional football had paid off.

It was a brief moment of joy though. All I'd done was secure the next couple of years and only then if I kept improving and performing.

First-team football was still a long way off so I had to knuckle down because an apprenticeship was no good if it didn't lead to a professional contract.

I'd only completed stage one, but for now though it felt good. I'd achieved something I desperately wanted. The youth players who were laughing at me when I arrived at the club now respected me. I'd been watching Ian Wright and Mark Bright at Palace for years and now I had a chance to emulate them.

That was my new dream.

~OWEN THE BOY WONDER ~

My progress once I'd signed that youth team contract was rapid. The pressure on me had been eased and I had some security.

We had a good youth team at Palace while I was there and I soon became the main man. I scored regularly and generally played pretty well, holding my own comfortably against the bigger London clubs who had the pick of the capital's players.

My reward, of course, had been a shock first team debut and a professional contract, but I was still eligible for youth team football and I was happy to keep playing for them.

In my second year as an apprentice, Palace went on a fantastic run in the FA Youth Cup and we reached the semi-finals.

Liverpool would be our opponents which was good for me as I'd supported them as a boy (I owned the Candy-sponsored strip) and we fancied our chances.

The first leg was at Anfield and we were confident of causing an upset. Most of those hopes rested on me, the team's best player and top scorer.

We had Hayden Mullins and Clinton Morrison in our side as well, but I was the man. I already had a pro contract in my pocket, I'd already played in the First Division so I expected Liverpool to know all about me.

I did score at Anfield with a fantastic lob, but I was overshadowed by a 16 year-old kid on the other side. We'd heard how good Michael Owen was, but we didn't realise how good.

He opened the scoring, I equalised, but then he just ran riot. He wasn't just quick, he was intelligent, he linked up play and his finishing was brilliant.

Jamie Carragher was also in that Liverpool side, but Owen, despite being much smaller than everyone else, was the best player on the pitch by some distance.

He scored a brilliant hat-trick at Anfield in a 3-1 win and then another hat-trick in the second leg at Selhurst Park, a game I missed because of injury.

The second leg finished 4-4, but Liverpool were never in danger of losing the tie. If they needed a goal Owen would deliver one.

I thought I was good, but Owen was on a different planet. I may have been a member of the Palace first-team squad, but I realised how far I still had to go to make a success of my career.

~ KUNG FU CANTONA ~

During my apprenticeship at Palace, I also caught a glimpse of what could happen to highly-strung players in this highly-pressurised world of professional football.

Towards the end of the 1994-95 season Manchester United came to play Palace at Selhurst Park.

I watched the game with the rest of the youth team from our normal spot near the dug outs. It wasn't a great game, but it exploded into life when United's Eric Cantona got involved in a spat with Richard Shaw and he was shown a red card.

Cantona reluctantly left the pitch and was walking along the touchline towards the dressing room when he stopped suddenly. You are quite close to the stands as you walk down the touchline at Selhurst Park and you could hear everything, abuse as well as acclaim, raining down from the stands.

As you can imagine, Cantona was getting dog's abuse from our fans as he walked towards the dressing room. Actually, Cantona never walked, he strutted and swaggered, but all of a sudden he stopped and fixed his stare on someone in the crowd.

The next thing I saw was Cantona jumping into the stand and drop-kicking one of the Palace fans who had charged down the steps to holler at him.

It was a beautiful karate kick followed by a fantastic punch. I was already in awe of Cantona's playing ability and my respect for him had now doubled – not because I advocate beating up fans – but because he clearly wouldn't take shit from anyone.

The boxer in me makes me want to defend myself at all times although Cantona did take it to an extreme level and received a long ban for his troubles.

But some fans get away with murder with some of the things they shout at footballers. Inside I was quietly pleased that a player, a top player at that, had made a stand.

~ THE END IS NIGH ~

I was doing okay under Coppell the second time around. He was good to me and always explained why I wasn't playing, but that he still rated me and my chance would come.

Coppell had an impossible job because the club was now skint, but the lads pulled together for him. Ray Lewington was coaching us and was the best I ever worked with.

I got my chance under Coppell in the 1999-2000 season and had a nice little run of three goals in four games, scoring against QPR, Port Vale and Nottingham Forest.

I was playing alongside Matt Svensson, who would later play with me at Norwich, and then alongside my mate Clinton Morrison and we had Mikael Forssel at the club as well.

Hayden Mullins was just making a name for himself in the first team, but we were just ticking along making sure we never went near the relegation zone.

We finished 15th - which was a good effort under the circumstances. I only managed one more goal, but I was playing and gaining valuable experience, but then a new chairman arrived.

Simon Jordan had an orange suit on when I first met him. That was weird and it didn't exactly make for a great first impression.

It did hint at a man who wasn't shy and didn't care too much about what people thought about him. It proved an accurate assessment of his character.

Predictably, Jordan made himself a high-profile chairman. He also wanted his own men around him so Coppell was soon out and Alan Smith came back to Selhurst Park as manager, a decision that suggested the new chairman wasn't that knowledgeable about football.

Jordan didn't say a lot to the likes of me, but he did speak with certain players who became part of his clique, but replacing Coppell with Smith wasn't a popular move as far as the vast majority of the first-team squad were concerned.

Smith had managed Palace before and led them to the First Division title, but he had a reputation as a long-ball manager and the game had moved on a bit by the time he returned.

Smith was the sort of bloke who dressed up in a snappy suit to come to the football ground. He'd never be without a Rolex on his wrist and in my opinion he used to be more interested in looking sharp than he was in putting on a decent training session.

He knew more about fashion than his job. I didn't rate him and I wasn't the only one. I was only a youngster, but even I could see through him so it was obvious he wasn't going to have the respect of the senior players.

I didn't think Smith couldn't coach to save his life. Dave Kemp was the brains in that department in Smith's time at Selhurst Park.

Smith would roll up to training with shorts on, displaying his pathetic, skinny legs and just fiddle about with his Rolex while Kemp did all the coaching.

In my opinion he was just a joker. It didn't help that he couldn't get our names right. He'd call George Ndah 'Bruce' and he'd call Bruce Dyer 'Dean' presumably because we all looked the same to him.

As a football person, Smith was a waste of time. As a man?

Well, I actually pity him.

In my opinion he could shout, but he couldn't coach. In my opinion he tried to bully people, but no-one took any notice. My big bust-up came soon after he took over and soon after I'd found God.

I had become a born-again Christian. The players were aware of this and there was soon some stick flying my way, but that was just dressing room and training ground banter so it wasn't a problem.

My true friends, Hayden Mullins, Bruce Dyer etc, were brilliant with me. They knew why I had gone down this path and they respected and supported my decision.

Smith was different and it came to a head when we went away for a week when we didn't have a game. The lads were allowed out one night towards the end of the week and I refused to go.

It was certain to end in a strip club or somewhere equally degrading and that was now against what I believed in.

The coaching staff heard about this and called me over. I explained I didn't believe in the drinking, messing around with women sort of stuff anymore and that I'd rather go to my room and relax.

I was big into team spirit and bonding sessions and realised that they were important to a team's success, but I also didn't think missing one night out would matter too much.

Smith didn't agree and this dinosaur couldn't understand the reasons I had given him. He didn't so much rant and rave as take the piss and he didn't stop.

I had felt unwanted by him anyway and that was confirmed by a place on the substitutes' bench for all but about four games when he was manager.

The team were losing most games, but I couldn't get a sniff apart from the very occasional start. It was clear he didn't rate me and that was confirmed when he called me into his office about a week after the week away.

"Lee," he said. "I've had an offer of £25,000 from Peterborough for you and I've accepted it. I want you to go and talk to them."

My jaw dropped to the floor. He was now definitely taking the piss. That was a pittance for me and I was better than that. I didn't see myself as a Second Division player either.

I'd done six years at Palace. My heart was there. I'd never left the area. I knew about Peterborough because I'd done well on loan there and I'd had a good time under a manager, Barry Fry, who I had a lot of time for, but I didn't want to go there permanently. I was a London boy. I had never moved away and even when I had been on loan it had been with a view to me coming back with some first-team games under my belt and being nearer to getting into the Palace first team.

But now we had this prat of a man judging me because of my lifestyle and my faith. This was personal as they could have got more than £25,000 for me and I could definitely have played at a higher standard.

I could never forgive Smith for what he did. My career had been ticking over nicely and now I was expected to take a huge step backwards.

I went to Peterborough because it meant getting away from this manager I didn't like. It was a reluctant move, but at least I would be going to a place where I would be loved and away from this awful manager and person, in my opinion.

It actually turned into a good one for my career, but it was a very sad end for my time at Palace.

I'd scored on my debut for the club at the age of 17 and now almost five years to the day I had been told to leave.

My last game for Palace was as a half-time substitute in a 1-0 home defeat by Sheffield United. I came on for Paul Kitson and played alongside Clinton Morrison.

I'd started just over 50 games for the club and come on a substitute almost the same number of times.

I felt unfulfilled when I left. I wanted to get them back into the Premier League, not leave them when they were struggling at the wrong end of Division One, something that wasn't likely to change with Smith in charge.

CHAPTER 11

'POSH AND PROUD'

I'd played for Barry Fry at Peterborough United on loan from Crystal Palace in the 1998-99 season and had got on well with him and everyone else at the club.

You hear lots of stories about Barry being a bit of a clown and playing up to the crowd a lot, but he was a popular figure in football and I liked him.

He didn't pretend he could coach like Terry Venables or motivate like Sir Alex Ferguson. He didn't try and make you believe he was as intelligent as Steve Coppell.

In fact it was obvious straight away that he had little clue about tactics or coaching, so he kept things simple which was often a good idea around footballers.

He used to watch training with his shirt off and his big belly hanging over his shorts. At least I think he was watching training as he used to spend most of his time on his mobile phone, no doubt cooking up his next deal.

Barry used to let his coaches coach and he'd then pick the team. It was usually 4-4-2 as he didn't like to complicate things, but he did insist that we all charged forward and tried to score as many goals as we could which suited me.

To be fair to Barry, he must have had something because he won a few promotions in his career. He gave a few good players their chance as well like Jimmy Bullard.

Sometimes, his job at training would be to hold the watch to time all the runs and stuff. If he was in a bad mood, which wasn't very often, he'd stop the sessions and make us do push-ups while calling us all sorts of rude names.

It wasn't funny at the time, but whenever I think back to those days with Barry and Peterborough it's hard not to chuckle.

I was 20 when I first went to play at Peterborough on loan and I loved every minute of it. Scoring twice on my debut at Cardiff helped especially as they were two cracking goals that helped the team come back from a goal down to win 3-1.

That was a big win for the team as they had started the season as one of the promotion favourites and yet they had lost at home in their first game.

The local press knives were apparently out for Barry – I'd been warned by some of the lads that the local reporter was a bit of a snake and not to be trusted – so I was pleased I could play my part to take the pressure off.

Barry played me up front with Jimmy Quinn and Martin Carruthers on my debut and we had Simon Davies and Steve Castle in the side so we were not likely to struggle for goals.

Quinn was just a legend. He was almost 40 when I met him, but he never missed the target in training or in a match and he was a top lad, really funny.

We didn't do so well in my next two games and I didn't score, but we smashed Exeter 4-1 at home on a Bank Holiday Monday and we were brilliant.

We actually fell behind, but I scored to make it 3-1 before half-time. Unfortunately, I tweaked a hamstring as I scored and went straight off the pitch.

That meant going straight back to Palace, but Barry was back on the phone as soon as he found out I was fit again so I returned to London Road for a second spell on loan a couple of months later. I don't know why he wanted me because they won a game 9-1 at

Barnet as soon as I left, but Barry didn't believe it was possible to have too many strikers!

It was during the second loan spell that I enjoyed my most memorable game for Peterborough as we beat Cambridge 2-1 at home.

It was a derby and Cambridge had been flying along mainly because of the goals being scored by Trevor Benjamin.

Before that night I'd heard a lot about this kid, but I'd never seen him play. I didn't want him to be the best striker on the pitch that night as that was going to be me.

I was in pretty good form myself at the time (I scored nine goals in 15 games in two different spells on loan that season) so I was in a confident, cocky mood.

I bumped into Benjamin on the pitch before that game and looked him up and down, stared him out and in my head I told him that I was going to be the main man that night. I often used big name opposition players to motivate me and Benjamin had a massive reputation as a kid in the lower divisions.

Benjamin also had a funny eye and I couldn't tell whether he was looking at me or staring at someone in the crowd, but he got the message.

Benjamin showed off his power and pace to open the scoring that night, but I got the winner and stole the headlines like I intended. Simon Davies played the ball through and I finished with my left foot. Steve Castle had equalised for us and there were over 10,000 in the ground that night generating a tremendous atmosphere.

That was the night I announced to the football world that I'd arrived. I made that night my own, while Benjamin was substituted before the end.

It was a big statement for a young player with not many games under his belt to make in what was a massive match in the area and in the division. I found the derby atmosphere and a big crowd a motivation, just as I had when scoring on my Palace debut.

In my loan spell at London Road I played with Davies and Matthew Etherington and you could tell that even as teenagers they were both destined for great things.

Barry loved to pick his kids and tell the world how great they were. It might have been a selling tactic, but it also gave younger players a great boost to read those sorts of headlines.

Davies just oozed class. He was a quiet, humble kid, but the rest of the lads could see his quality. He used to glide across the turf, but he could wallop a shot at goal from any distance with amazing accuracy.

Etherington was just 17 when I went there and he was just rapid, but he had the ball under control at all times.

There was a dearth of left-sided attacking players in the country when Matthew first came to the fore so he was soon being tipped for stardom at the highest level.

Those two lads benefitted from playing for Barry as youngsters. Barry wasn't scared to throw kids in if he thought they were good enough and he also let them express themselves.

They were basically given licence to play and they revelled in it. Barry also sold them at the right time when they were ready to play in the Premier League rather than letting them go too early when they would have been lost at a big club.

Barry understood how to motivate all sorts of players whether they were rookies making their way or senior players having a bad time.

Not everyone took to him, but I did. When I quit full-time football, he sent me a note to wish me a happy retirement. It was a neat touch from a good man.

He only really shouted at me in front of the other players on one occasion, but if you did the business for him he would look after you and he certainly looked after me.

I saw Barry throw the kitchen sink verbally at Andy Edwards once after a game which was strange as Andy was his captain, a real good lad and a strong player.

His team-talks were basically a load of swear words thrown together, but he was so passionate about the game I couldn't help but like him.

I also rated Martin Carruthers. He was great to play alongside. He wasn't the most naturally gifted striker, but he did a lot of hard work off the ball, the stuff that fans don't always appreciate. I returned to Palace at the end of the loan spells feeling good about myself. I was feeling less good when I came back, but Barry soon perked me up.

After Palace accepted the derisory £25,000 offer from Peterborough to make the move permanent, I went to meet Barry at the club to discuss personal terms.

His coach Wayne Turner was there as was the club secretary, Julie Etherington, the mum of Matthew Etherington. Matthew had moved on with Davies to Spurs midway through the previous season and yet Peterborough had still won promotion which was kind of impressive.

Barry offered me £1500 per week plus a £10,000 signing on fee, nothing ridiculous really, plus a bit of relocation money.

It was only a slight increase on what I was getting at Palace, but I wasn't a greedy man (the most I ever earned was about £10,000 a week when playing in the Premier League with Norwich) and the drop down a division was more of a worry.

Peterborough had just been promoted, but they weren't one of the favourites to go up again and I didn't want to become a good lower division footballer. I wanted to be a Premier League player again.

Barry was a very persuasive character and he just told me that if I banged in some goals for Peterborough he wouldn't stand in my way if a bigger club came in for me, which he was confident they would.

I trusted him. I'd seen Etherington and Davies had moved on to Spurs so if something similar happened to me I'd be more than happy.

Barry guaranteed I'd play every game and he would set up the side to get the best out of me. I believed him and I developed the mindset that I would move to Peterborough, score my goals and that would help Barry, the club and me.

Barry understood all that. He knew that above all else I just wanted to play football and get on in my career. He certainly had the contacts in the game to get bigger clubs interested in me.

I signed for him and it turned out to be a great move, and I was thrilled when I was inducted into the Posh Hall of Fame with the ceremony taking place just before a match with Palace earlier this year.

I had originally been insulted when Palace told me which club they wanted to sell me to, but Barry's positive approach and the reception and welcome I received from the fans changed my mind instantly.

Barry just let me play my football as he knew I'd do the business for him if my mind wasn't cluttered with too many instructions.

I felt I would be quick and strong enough to score plenty of goals at this level and it was goal-scorers that the top clubs wanted to sign.

Barry rarely tried to advise me and when he bollocked me it usually ended with him telling me what a great player I was! He'd be forever bigging me up in the press, probably because he wanted to sell me.

Some people in the squad hated him, but I didn't. He threw the odd tea cup and swore a lot when things weren't going so well, but he never bore a grudge.

It was a good time in my career, the goals were flowing and I was playing well in a good team, that at the start included quality players like David Farrell, even though he always seemed to be miserable, and Adam Drury.

Barry once gave me a week off when my child was ill and I loved him for that. This was a bloke I wanted to play for and it showed in my performances.

Barry played me up front with Andy Clarke and Jason Lee at different times. Clarkey was a lovely bloke and for someone who had played at the top level in the country for Wimbledon, he was very quiet and unassuming.

He was so laid back it was just untrue and he gave me one of the biggest laughs of my career when he failed a drugs test.

He'd actually gone missing for a while and no-one knew where he was, but then the news broke about this drugs test he'd failed. It showed traces of marijuana.

Clarkey came back to the club and said it must have been some dodgy cake that he'd eaten after his sister had brought it back from Amsterdam. His sister even told him it was called 'weed cake', but Andy still scoffed it down and thought nothing of it until he failed the drugs test.

It was the worst excuse any of us had ever heard and we just fell about laughing. Andy would just smile and shrug his shoulders, but his excuse worked as he got quite a short ban.

He could turn it on as a player when in the mood, and when he managed to stay onside, while Jason Lee was just a monster, but also a better player than people realised.

I remember Jason giving me the eye when I first turned up at the club. He reckoned I had a swagger and that I would have to play well to justify and I hope I did.

I hit it off straight away with Jason. We became firm friends and we are still close today. He was the best man at my wedding to Sofia.

He was a useful ally on the pitch as well. I could look after myself, but when Jason was playing I didn't have to.

There were some massive defenders at that level and we had one called Simon Rea. I used to call him 'Dumpling' but he had good feet and was a decent footballer.

Simon had one physical deformity that creased the lads up every time they saw it. Simon's party trick was to get his abnormally-sized ball bag out at every opportunity and it really was one of the weirdest-looking things I've ever seen.

I was also good friends with Dennis Pearce. Dennis, who is a teacher now, was a real joker and we are still in touch.

I tore up the Second Division. I was up against some people who would kick me, but I could hold my own and I don't think defenders at that level enjoyed playing against me because I couldn't be bullied.

We lost my first game back at the club at Brentford, but we beat Notts County in my first home match and I scored my first goal as a full-time Posh player when we came from behind to beat Colchester.

I scored reasonably regularly that season, but more importantly I stayed fit. I played 45 games that season (2000-01) for Palace and Posh, and scored 13 goals, all of them for Posh having joined the club in October.

Nothing really happened for the team in my three years at Peterborough. There were no pushes for promotion and we never really threatened to get relegated.

I was pleased with my form and became a fans' favourite because I scored goals and because I worked my socks off in every match. I became well known for my 't' shirt celebrations as well. I'd lift my shirt up after scoring goals to show off pictures of my son Kasey and my sister Tracey.

Posh actually started really well in my second season at the club. We even hammered QPR 4-1 in one of the best team performances I've ever been involved in.

I missed the first five matches of the season with a little injury, but I scored the only goal of the game on my re-appearance at Chesterfield.

We then beat Cambridge and thrashed Bournemouth 6-0. Our next game was against Blackpool at home and I was left on the substitutes' bench.

To this day I don't know why Barry did that, but we went 2-0 down in about 15 minutes so he sent me on. I scored straight away, we got back to 2-2 and then I scored a last-minute winner. If Barry dropped me to give me a kick up the backside it worked and next up were QPR whom everyone assumed would win the league.

We conceded an early goal, but we then really tore into them. David Farrell was flying and we gave a quality defender like Dan Shittu such a hard time he was eventually sent off.

Farrell equalised and I scored early in the second-half, but we completely battered them for basically the entire 90 minutes. I walked off the pitch that night thinking, 'wow, we could go places this season as few teams will be better than QPR.'

Jimmy Bullard was playing for us then and what a midfielder he was. He turned up at the club with another quality footballer Tom Williams from West Ham reserves and Barry had clearly worked his magic in the transfer market again by finding two gems.

Mark Tyler was our goalkeeper and only a lack of height stopped him going right to the top and I was playing up front with a real brainy player in Neale Fenn.

The dressing room was buzzing after we beat QPR, but we then went to Bury, played crap, lost and we were never the same again. I was still getting my goals, but the season fizzled out for the team apart from some excitement in the FA Cup.

I scored in a replay against Darlington which got us through to play Newcastle at home in front of the TV cameras.

What a great game that was as we came back from 2-0 down to get level before a controversial penalty given against me, helped Newcastle to win 4-2.

The referee decided that I handled a ball that I wasn't even looking at and awarded Newcastle a penalty. There is not a cat in hell's chance that spot-kick would have been awarded at the other end.

That game again showed our potential as a team because the likes of Alan Shearer and Sir Bobby Robson admitted they were scared when David Farrell equalised midway through the second half.

Later in the season I did claim the first hat-trick of my career in a 5-0 win over Tranmere and I was chuffed when I scored twice in the final game of the season against Bury to reach 20 goals, the first time I had ever achieved that.

That sort of form in a team that finished 17th (four places lower than the previous season) had started to attract the interest of bigger clubs.

Norwich had certainly started paying attention to me, so I was keen to impress when Peterborough played them in a pre-season friendly. Instead I left the game on a stretcher as I suffered the worst injury of my career.

No-one was to blame, I just landed awkwardly, broke and badly dislocated my ankle. I remember Andy Clarke and Francis Green (a young striker who should have done much better in the game) telling me not to look down, but I did and my foot was facing the wrong way.

I don't know why, but I picked the foot up and forced it back to where it should have been. I was in agony, but I was told later that what I did might have saved my career, so a six-month lay-off didn't seem too bad.

I'd suffered like Michael Owen early in his career with hamstring pulls, but I'd got over them and now suffered something much worse.

I was gutted that the injury meant the end of Norwich's interest in me, but I was determined not to let it beat me. I worked so hard to get back and I think the team were pleased to see me when I did return.

The team won the first game of the season at Luton without me, but then they went seven games without scoring and slumped to the bottom of the table.

I came back on Boxing Day as a substitute and we grabbed a draw at Colchester with a late goal, but I wasn't ready and sat out another couple of months.

Jason Lee and Andy Clarke were scoring the goals for us as we climbed out of trouble and by the time I came back we had moved away from danger.

I managed five goals in 10 games in the last few weeks of the season including one when we lost 6-1 at Plymouth. Sagi Burton was taken off at half-time and he was so pissed off with events he smashed a window in the changing room and a Plymouth steward called the police!

It wasn't that serious. The club paid for the damage and the front page headlines the next day were soon forgotten.

I also scored in a game against Wigan in bizarre fashion. I was sent on as a substitute, scored a goal that got us a draw and was then taken off injured.

Paul Showler was the club physio then and when he was taking me off he told me that I was too good for this level and that I would soon be moving on, but how he knew that on a 12-minute performance I have no idea!

It was important to me though that I reminded people I was still around and now I was determined to start the following season well.

It wasn't that I was desperate to leave Posh as I enjoyed it there with some great people like Jason Lee and Jimmy Bullard. Bullard just never shut up and was always playing pranks on his team-mates, the staff and basically anybody who crossed his path, but he was such a positive influence and a great player at that level, we all indulged him.

Bullard left for Wigan midway through that 2002-03 season which surprised no-one as he had Premier League written all over him and that was where Wigan were heading. The team did well without him though and we were happy enough with an 11th place finish considering the disastrous start we had suffered.

I started slowly the following season, but luckily I hit a purple patch around October/November and I struck 10 goals in 10 games.

The team weren't winning many games though and we were stuck near the bottom for most of the first-half of the season.

I did score a last-minute winner in a big game against Wycombe who were also struggling, but my time at Posh was now coming to an end.

I was playing well and, no disrespect to Posh as I loved playing for them and my relationship with the fans was superb, but I knew I was ready to play for a bigger club at a higher level.

I did think that club would be Wigan. I'd had a couple of conversations with their manager Paul Jewell. They were a club with a rich owner who were on the march through the divisions and I must admit the chance to play again with Bullard was a big temptation.

I also learnt that Spurs were after me, but Barry got too excited and asked for too much money. I was unhappy at the time as that would have been a fantastic move for a London boy, but I was soon on the move.

In January, 2004 Barry called me into his office and said Norwich were interested in signing me again and he'd agreed to sell me for £325,000.

He said he didn't want to lose me, but the club needed the cash so he had no choice. It was a £300,000 profit for the club which pleased me as I wanted Posh to do well.

Barry told me I was to go and see Norwich manager Nigel Worthington that day. He could have held me back I guess, but he didn't so I'll always be grateful for that.

I was excited. I'd played at a good standard at Palace, but I was a much better player now. I'd matured as a footballer and a person, and the drop down a division had worked out great for me.

I felt I was a proper goal-scorer now, but I had nothing left to prove at Posh.

My last game for Posh was a Johnstone's Paint Trophy defeat at local rivals Northampton.

The players used to hate that competition, but we had to field a good side against the local rivals.

I equalised in the 90th minute, but we lost in extra-time and I was strangely subdued in what was effectively a very low-key game.

It was a sad way to leave a club that I still love dearly, but now was the time to move on.

I borrowed a silver Range Rover from a friend, grabbed my agent Tim Webb and headed for Norwich.

CHAPTER 12

'WOMEN HAVE BEEN MY DOWN FALL'

I inherited many things from my dad. His sporting prowess, his dedication to his profession, his refusal to give up when things are going badly and the fact that he was a real ladies man have all been passed down the family line.

I know which one has caused me the most grief.

Women played a huge part in my downfall. Since my secondary school days, the ladies have always liked me and I've taken advantage of that with affairs and one-night stands all the way through my life.

That has led to many situations I wish I could have avoided.

I was 16 when I met Ness, whom went on to become my first wife. I'd just finished school and I met her at my dad's gym in Herne Hill.

I first clocked her when she was talking to my dad. We glanced at each other, I liked what I saw and I had enough self-confidence to talk to her.

I wasn't shy so I wondered over. I worked my charm on her and we started going out. I told my mates I was going out with an older woman (she claimed she was 21) and they loved it as it was quite a coup for a youngster to date mature women back in those days.

I remember speaking to her on the phone one day at a time when I wasn't happy at home. I was living with my dad and his young girlfriend and I didn't feel comfortable having someone just a few years older than me trying to act as my mum.

Ness pounced when she heard this. I'd stayed at her place a few times and she just suggested I move in with her permanently. Wow, how exciting I thought at the time, but now I regret rushing into such a life-changing decision.

I didn't even consider the realities of taking on the responsibility of someone else's child for instance. Ness had a son from a previous relationship, Jordan who was a good kid.

So there I was at 17 taking on the role of a dad. I was shopping for groceries and generally doing domestic stuff, but there were physical benefits so it seemed to me that I was getting a good deal.

We had Kasey when I was 18 and that was a real blessing for both of us. My reaction to my first born was the same as my dad's had been to his.

I was so proud of Ness and of Kasey. Many people told me I was mad to have a kid when I was still a teenager myself, but I wanted to be the perfect father from day one.

This was a big deal for me. My own father had influenced my life in so many positive ways and I wanted to do as well for Kasey.

Unfortunately being a good, strong, reliable husband was proving far more difficult. As time passed by, I started to get attention from other women and I was easily tempted. I was older now and I was feeling trapped in my relationship. I wanted to explore other possibilities and that led me to stray.

Offers became too hard to turn down. I was immature, I guess, although nothing interfered with my love for Kasey who was always in my thoughts.

Ness hated me going out as she was insecure and with good reason. She after all knew how old she really was and she knew I already had a reputation with the ladies.

I did get confused by my behaviour though and it was around

this time that I started going to church. That calmed me down carnally.

In fact the church decided that living in sin was indeed a sin, so I was bounced into a marriage that I really didn't want.

I thought I did. I told myself that Ness had given me a beautiful son so I owed it them both to make the marriage work.

Just as importantly in my head I was trying to do the right thing by Jesus. I even moved out of Ness's flat for a few months and stopped sleeping with her before the wedding as I was told it was the right thing to do.

We were rushed into marriage so much it took place in Croydon Registry Office in the middle of the football season.

Her real age came out at our wedding. Ness was eight years older than me and this took me aback. If she was prepared to lie about something trivial like her age, what else would I find out in the future.

From day one of our relationship Vanessa had been lying. Finding out, especially on my wedding day, that she'd deceived me about her age for four years was horrible.

Perhaps she had ulterior motives for doing what she did.

Before the service, I was sitting there looking particularly unhappy for someone who was about to get wed to the mother of my child and dad picked up on this. 'Champ' he said 'it's not too late to pull out'.

He was right of course. I was clearly having second thoughts and in my heart of hearts I knew this was going to be a rocky marriage. But I couldn't face hurting Kasey's mum at this late stage so I went through with it and what a big, expensive mistake that turned out to be.

We did have a lovely little honeymoon, but Ness quickly became very possessive. She had a fiery temperament.

I went on the one lads' holiday of my life to Tenerife with Bruce Dyer, Shaun Newton and Richard Rufus, another friend from the football world. We went there to watch Spoony who was DJ-ing over there, but my phone just did not stop ringing.

Leon McKenzie

Every day, Ness would call and say, or usually shout, that she didn't trust me and that my stuff would be out on the street when I got back.

When drunk, Ness turned into this nasty, vindictive person. She was loud, she'd show off and she would often try and humiliate me in company.

We had lots of fights. Some became physical, but not on my part as I would never, ever lay hands on a woman.

One time, she threw a glass that hit my back and smashed causing me to bleed all over the place. Switch that scenario around and imagine that I had caused her to bleed and all hell would rightly break loose, but as it was a woman committing the abuse it didn't seem to matter.

In my opinion, her aggression pushed me into more affairs. My love for Ness was being lost amid all the tension and I was growing apart from her.

I was also maturing. I wasn't this 17 year-old boy awestruck by an older woman any more. I didn't want to be with her, but I also didn't want to leave my son so I carried on with the pretence, while finding some comfort elsewhere.

Ness, Jordan and Kasey, had come with me when I left London for Peterborough, but things weren't good. I quickly had an affair, two actually, with a couple of sisters.

I met Daniella on a night out. We used to go down to Ferry Meadows car park for fun- in fact we'd go anywhere.

She was spontaneous and exciting. One time she called to tell me she had the keys to a boxercise gym in the city and asked me to meet her there.

When I arrived, she was waiting for me in the middle of the boxing ring. She looked very seductive and clearly wasn't in the mood for fighting.

Daniella was great, but she made the mistake of introducing me to her sister Emma. I started seeing Emma as well. Not surprisingly Daniella found out.

She was heartbroken, but me and Emma carried on until one

fateful day when Ness found out about my behaviour. Ness was at Heritage Park School waiting for Kasey when one of the other mums told her about me and Emma.

I had no idea that Ness knew, so I went merrily about my business which meant seeing Emma on a regular basis.

But I was pretty sure Ness had discovered my guilty secret when I drove home after a night with Emma in the early hours of one morning.

I had a Mercedes back then and a big house on the Park Farm Estate on the outskirts of Peterborough with a long driveway. I pulled in and I could see Ness prowling about just outside the house and it looked like she had a hammer in her hand.

My heart started thumping, and not in a romantic way. What could I make up? How could I explain this away? Nothing came to mind even though I drove as slowly as possible to let my head catch up with my heart.

Eventually I pulled up. Ness came storming towards me screaming 'Who's Emma, who's Emma?' It was indeed a hammer in her hand and she was now holding it above her head.

She didn't wait to hear me answer her question either and the hammer came down on the windscreen, shattering glass all over me and the driveway.

I was now in full panic mode. I'd been driving for years and yet I couldn't find reverse and she was hammering away at the car, the windows, and the bodywork.

The neighbours had come out by now and for want of my failure to think of anything else to do, I lit up a cigarette and tried to stay as cool as possible. I'm not sure it worked.

There was no way I was going back into that house. When Ness had finished her handiwork, I managed to locate reverse and creep slowly down the drive and away from her until things calmed down.

I went back eventually, but instead of telling her the truth that I'd fallen out of love with her, we patched things up and we compromised which involved me giving up Emma.

Emma was now pissed off as well as broken hearted. A little while after I joined Norwich, she sent me a two-page letter telling me how much she missed me.

It was flattering to have so many women chasing me, but I'm so glad my life is less complicated now.

Emma was too late anyway. I was with Sofia by then.

When I moved from Peterborough to Norwich, Ness again came with me in the hope of a fresh start, but even though I was now earning good money, for some reason this made her worse.

She seemed to be drinking more and she had become even more insecure.

The footballers' wives would sit together at games and Ness would hear about how much players like Darren Huckerby were on and demand to know why I earned less.

I used to give her £600 per month spending money, but that wasn't enough for her. She'd ridicule the amount I gave her whenever friends came to the house, even though she hadn't worked a day in her life and she was saying all these things in the living room of a massive and beautiful house, the best I've ever owned.

One day, I'd had enough of her moaning and went shopping on my own. I had a blast, spending £5,000 or so on clothes for myself and when I got back to the house I laid everything out in front of Ness to see what she thought.

It was a bit provocative to be fair and sure enough Ness went off on one, shouting at me for spending so much without buying her a treat. I couldn't take this from a woman who used to spend so much time asleep, my team-mates would joke about the curtains being closed all day long.

I went outside and phoned my dad to say I was filing for a divorce. He backed me, but Ness fell pregnant with Mariya so I was trapped as I couldn't walk out on a newborn baby.

I stayed for another year. It wasn't exactly a happy home although it did become calmer for a while. My feelings for Ness had gone though. I was living a lie and I hated myself for it.

Eventually, I took Ness to a local restaurant to tell her we were finished. I told her my feelings for her were gone. I told her I cared about her, but I didn't love her.

I moved out the next day and into an apartment. It was bliss. I felt free and I couldn't believe how much I enjoyed the simple things like cooking for myself, as well as the peace and quiet.

Unfortunately, I applied for a divorce at the time I was earning the most money of my career. It was about to get expensive.

"I'm going to take you for every penny you have, and fuck up your life" Ness announced. And she went on to have a pretty good go at doing exactly that.

It also, quickly, became nasty. Ness soon realised that I had met Sofia. The reality that I'd moved on had now kicked in and she didn't like it. She lost the plot and became even more unpredictable.

One time Sofia and I came out of a shopping centre in Norwich to find our car had been blocked in, by Ness.

All of a sudden, this angry-faced figure popped out from nowhere and was charging at us. It was Ness and she looked furious.

So I gave Sofia the car keys and told her to go. We nipped off sharpish, but we both knew there would be other encounters.

Another time, Sofia and I were in Sainsbury's car park and Ness turned up as arranged to drop Kasey and Mariya off so they could spend some time with me.

Ness said she needed petrol money. I'd become fed up with this constant demand for cash, so I refused. She lost her head a bit and started shouting and swearing at me, but then Sofia snapped as well and chucked a £20 note at Ness.

I'd not seen Sofia like this before. I realised I had to get between them but my seatbelt jammed. Ness jumped out of her car first closely followed by Sofia who leapt out of ours. Ness started the fight by grabbing Sofia's hair, but Sofia fought back and when I finally got free and split them up Ness, who was a lot bigger than Sofia, was on the floor.

Blood was pouring out of her mouth, but Ness was a big woman and the tables could easily have been turned very quickly so it was a good job I got out in time to stop it there and then.

It was an awful time, never knowing when this woman would turn up and disrupt my life. She was also happy to use my kids to get at me, in my opinion.

Predictably, when we split up she messed me about regarding access with the kids. I'd turn up at the appointed time and the house would be empty which forced me to the courts just to make sure I saw my babies.

I remember scoring against Manchester United and being so happy the next day- I wanted to share it with my kids.

I went into the house and put Mariya on my lap, but Ness came in screaming 'get the fuck out of my house, if you don't leave the house now all hell will break loose.'

She was acting up again in company (Adam Newton, an old Peterborough team-mate was there with his partner) and before I knew it she'd slapped me hard across the face.

She knew I wouldn't hit her back so I put Mariya down and left. This woman was becoming dangerous.

Initially we tried to split up without using solicitors. I was giving Ness £2,000 a month which was okay as I was earning good money at the time and I was paying all the bills, but she was impossible.

About that time, Ray Parlour's missus went to court to divorce him and won a part of all Ray's future earnings. Ness clearly fancied a similar deal.

Ness didn't really understand the money side of things though. I was on good money, but nowhere as much as Ray Parlour would have been on!

We went to court, spending £100,000 on solicitors, before settling. There was no record of the money I'd been giving her and she denied I'd been as generous as I had.

She received a £42,000 lump sum and got to stay in the £360,000 house we'd been living in. She was also awarded £2,000 a month for the next four years which was a tidy sum.

When she wanted to move back to Peterborough, I bought her a house for £200,000 from David Farrell, an old team-mate of mine, which she moved into with the kids.

That divorce agreement took care of most of the money I'd earned from my time at Norwich, but clearly it wasn't enough.

~ PAPER TALK ~

I can take criticism, but don't dare suggest I don't love or care for my kids. Ness did just that, but not just privately, or to a few friends, but to the whole country in an article in a national publication.

I was driving home after a match early one Saturday evening when I took a call from a journalist asking me whether or not I wanted to comment on a story Vanessa had given them.

He gave me only vague details so I decided I didn't want anything to do with it other than to point out how generous I had actually been, but the supposed 'revelations' were horrible to read....

I picked up the paper the next morning and sat there stunned reading this 'story'.

Now most of this article was exaggerated bollocks, but I was more horrified at the effect it would have on our kids. She clearly hadn't thought about that when she took the money from the paper.

According to her, I didn't see them enough, I didn't give her enough money to feed them and they were living on scraps as there was no food in the house. My kids were starving because of me, but I apparently didn't care as I had a new woman.

Ness was trying to make me look as bad as possible. What she didn't realise she was that she was actually making herself look bad.

All my friends and family knew all our financial arrangements and they all knew my character would not let me treat my kids like she had claimed. Basically much of this was rubbish.

She certainly made no mention of the generous terms she received as part of our divorce agreement. If she had, people would have been able to judge us fairly, but that obviously wasn't the point of the article which was designed to embarrass me.

Before the court settlement, I had stopped giving her cash because I couldn't be sure what she was spending it on, but I'd go and do the grocery shopping for her. I'd carry five or six bags of stuff full of my kids' favourites and drop them off at the house. I was also covering every single bill.

I was fuming, but I took so many calls from people taking my side that day it cheered me up. They all believed she had come out of it worse than me.

The people that knew me, knew I would die for my babies. They knew I wasn't capable of doing what she was suggesting.

It always came down to money with Ness and it's still the same to this day.

Shortly after the newspaper article appeared, Ness also didn't help herself by appearing on one of those Footballers' wives programmes with Ian Walker's wife Suzi and others.

They were slagging off their lifestyle saying that it's not all it's cracked up to be as basically all footballers are cheats and liars.

I moved to Coventry from Norwich a couple of days later for a million quid (£600,000 plus add ons) so you can imagine the banter that came flying my way!

I'm not as wealthy as I was and I now pretty much live on my pension (I do own a couple of properties) and yet Ness is sadly still in a place where she relies on me financially.

Happily, she now has a couple of jobs and I am pleased for her because that helps everyone, but I wish she'd found work many years ago rather than wait until she's 42.

I can't give her what I haven't got. She gets a fair monthly amount considering my own circumstances, but I rang the Child Support Agency recently and they reckoned I'm paying her too much!

I don't have the lifestyle I used to have. I don't go out every weekend any more, but Ness still makes ridiculous demands.

I have to be fair to her and say that we created two gorgeous children together and it is obvious that both Kasey and Mariya love their mum very much.

I don't agree with how Vanessa conducts herself, but she also loves our two children and that's the most important thing right now.

For that I am grateful, but I'm never sure that it won't kick off again between us.

She has been known to run me down in front of my kids. I was in tears recently when I received a Facebook message from Kasey, my first-born.

He said I was 'a bit of a joke for the way I was treating his mother', that he 'hated seeing his mother so unhappy because I was apparently not paying her enough money.'

He was 15 so he couldn't possibly know, but those messages knocked me for six. They broke my heart.

Part of me wanted to box him, but I realised he'd just been poisoned by Vanessa's actions so I immediately jumped on the train to Norwich (they've moved back there now).

I was fresh out of prison. I was serving an 18-month driving ban, but I had to see Kasey and Mariyah immediately.

I explained to them both that although I still lived in a nice house I actually had a lot of debt, I had my own major problems and that I'd given their mum virtually everything I had.

I even showed them the divorce agreement which had all the figures on relating to what I'd given Ness.

As the reality of the situation kicked in, we were all soon crying, but they gave me a big hug and we were okay again.

What little respect I had left for Ness had gone now. She'd messed with my kids' heads, but it hadn't worked as me, Kasey and Mariya are closer than ever now.

The reality was that I'd failed in my marriage, but it was also a fact that I had been a 17 year-old boy moving in with a 25 year-old woman which was a bad move on both our parts.

I should have realised because I had experienced something similar when I moved from my mum's house to my dad's house when I was about 13. My dad was living with a younger woman back then and she was just a few years older than me.

I wouldn't blame my dad's girlfriend, but we were too close in age and I never felt comfortable. My dad's girlfriend was eight years older than me just like Ness was. This gap was too much.

I guess you live and learn the hard way. Ultimately, time has moved on, but it's all about my babies and making them comfortable. We have to stop all the bitterness especially where the money is concerned.

If my circumstances change for better or for worse so do hers. We split up eight years ago so we should be able to work together and communicate better for the sake of our two beautiful children.

I had the world at my feet at the age of 17 which was too much too soon. I then got married far too soon.

I hold my hands up to some of my affairs, but I was young and naive. My mum wasn't around at the time and I probably needed her to give me some good advice.

From the age of 17 I didn't have the same sort of life as the teenagers I grew up with. I regret the sex with Ness, but not the babies we had together as they are my world.

CHAPTER 13

'THE CHAMPS'

I was born in Mayday Hospital, Croydon at 12.40pm on May 17, 1978. I was a big baby, 8lbs 10ozs, born to Clinton McKenzie and his wife Donna.

Dad was a professional boxer. He was a three-time British Champion. I was his first child and at the first opportunity he raised me in his arms to the sky and thanked God for his first-born.

He said he knew I was going to be special from that day on. I hope I haven't let him down.

I was named after Leon Spinks the heavyweight boxer who once beat Mohammed Ali in a World title fight, but Dad has simply called me 'Champ' ever since I can remember.

Naturally, boxing has been a big part of my life since day one.

I could have become a professional boxer, but I found something I was better at and dad backed me all the way.

When I was born, dad was just starting his professional career. He'd fought as an amateur in the 1976 Olympics in Montreal for Great Britain and lost to a guy called Sugar Ray Leonard, who went on to become one of the greatest pro fighters of all time.

I've seen the tapes of the fight and my dad was amazing against such a massive talent – he did his country proud. I was in awe of him from a very early age and in many ways I still am.

Boxing didn't pay much when my dad eventually turned pro (he was on about £1,000 a fight in the early days) so he worked at the local Tesco as a security guard and mum held down two jobs.

We lived in a one-bedroom top floor flat (3 flights of stairs to get to it) at 17b, The Crescent, Thornton Heath, Surrey, which my parents had paid £5,900 to own.

It was sold for £7,000 four months later which was typical of my mum as she had a good business head.

We upgraded to a house at 17, Elm Road, Thornton Heath which is where I grew my first teeth at four months and learnt to walk aged 10 months so I was already a quick developer.

My mum worked as an estate agent (she also worked as a cleaner) so she knew the markets and she soon organised another move to an okay area near Norbury.

She sold the Elm Road house for £18,500 and we moved into 73 Headcorn Road.

My childhood was generally happy, at least in the early days. I soon had a sister, Rebecca, and there was a lot of love around from a big family. Dad was one of six brothers.

I was a lively child and I am amazed my sister still speaks to me as I used to practise all my Bruce Lee karate kicks and Rocky boxing moves on her!

I saw dad fight a few times and I loved it. I never felt he was in danger of getting hurt. He was a monster, a machine in the ring, to me he was unbeatable.

He retired at one point, but came back to win a British title at the age of 33 and he gave me the credit for his achievement. It was the second time he'd regained the light-welterweight title to make him a three-time champion in total.

Dad was a bit down before the fight against a formidable, and younger, opponent in Lloyd Christie. My parents had started having a few problems at home so he was sad and not confident about beating Lloyd who had been on the top of his game.

I wasn't supposed to be at the fight, but my granddad Fred

(mum's dad) had the idea to take me there to give dad a boost. He called my mum and after much pleading she agreed to let me go. My mum dressed me up in a smart shirt. I put a tie on and wore a long, tidy coat.

Granddad arranged for me to go into the dressing room before the fight. Dad was sitting there, head bowed, he looked as sad as I'd ever seen him.

I'll never forget the look in his eyes though when he saw me. Whatever was troubling him was forgotten in that instant, his eyes lit up and he snapped into a smile.

We touched gloves (well he had gloves on!), hugged, didn't say much, but he went out and won the fight. Afterwards, he said me turning up had given him the inspiration to fight well.

The first fight I can remember watching was his first GB title defence when he beat Steve Early. I jumped into the ring afterwards and he picked me up and threw me around a bit – they are happy memories of a great father.

Dad was a clever boxer, not really a big puncher, but a craftsman with style. Titles were boxed for over 15 rounds in his day and his three fights with Colin Powers, two defeats one win, were among the greatest ever domestic fights.

Non-boxing fans would watch those three fights and be converted. I understood what having heart was by watching my dad fight.

I could see he had nothing left towards the end of a bout, but he would keep fighting and he would find more.

That's the special quality of a true champion and made me respect my dad as a fighter, but more importantly as a man.

Bizarrely given my dad's reputation I had to step in and save him once.

Dad and pubs never really worked and it almost went horribly wrong when he purchased one called 'The Prince of Wales' in Thornton Heath and re-named it 'McKenzie's'.

This pub was in a bad area where drug dealing was rife. Many used to use Dad's pub and he banned them all.

But one big bully of a man was not taking no for an answer. Dad had caught him smoking weed and threw him out, but as I pulled up outside the pub in my car I could see he wasn't going to leave. Dad was getting on a bit by now and this guy was big. He was mugging my dad off and then he stood up and put his hand on my dad.

I wasn't having that and lets just say the man was dealt with.

About a week later in the barber shop I was thanked by several local residents for getting rid of a bad man from the area.

My dad gave up the pub soon afterwards. There was just too much drug dealing in the neighbourhood and he had become very uncomfortable.

The early days with my parents were comfortable. We lived near to the Crystal Palace FC ground.

There were no problems with race at first. Asians, black kids and white kids all mixed happily. We had holidays abroad, we had a bit of money and the schools I attended were fine.

I could be boisterous when the mood took me. I was also adventurous which nearly killed me on one holiday in Spain when I decided I could swim even though I'd never been taught.

I walked straight into the pool, took on the deep end and had to be rescued as swimming didn't come naturally to me then. I was four or five at the time.

It was one of those things I did that were hard to explain. I've had a few more like that in my life.

~ I WANTED TO BE PELE ~

Pele inspired me to start playing football.

Not because of his great performances for Brazil, but because of the film 'Escape to Victory'. I was a big Rocky fan as well and Sylvester Stallone was in the football film about British prisoners of war beating their Nazi captors.

Michael Caine was in it as were Bobby Moore, Ossie Ardiles and an entire Ipswich Town squad.

I loved that film, but Pele was the man. When he scored the

winning goal with an overhead kick, I decided that's what I wanted to do in my life.

If being the best at football could get you a part in a film alongside Stallone then I wanted to do it!

I was straight into the back garden throwing a tennis ball up in the air and doing over-head kicks past an imaginary goalkeeper. I was only five or six at the time, but I became obsessed with football.

I'd been decent at judo and I'd been good at boxing and, ironically given the incident in Spain, I was also a good swimmer. I realised I could run fast by playing British Bulldogs in the school playground!

I also became captain of the school athletics team.

I won a few judo competitions, but the sport never really gripped me so I binned it. I had reached brown belt status when I quit.

My first football club was Alpha FC. I was a central midfielder at the time and I loved playing for my manager Ian.

I was like a little terrier, darting about all over the place. I found it easy to ghost past people, but I was creating goals more than I was scoring them.

I loved the game, I loved learning and improving. I started to win trophies like most improved player, followed by player of the year.

I played in the playground at Winterbourne School with a tennis ball. Some of the talent on show was amazing.

I played for the school team as a left back. My PE teacher, Mr Bone, was one of the first big influences on my career. I loved a tackle and playing in all these different positions at an early age definitely helped me develop quickly as a player.

Winterbourne reached a cup final once which led to my first appearance at Selhurst Park. We lost against a top quality private school, but I played well and the buzz at playing at that stadium was brilliant.

I'd tell myself that I'd be back there playing for Palace one day.

When you played for the school, all the pupils and teachers were behind you. If you scored a goal, the school basically erupted as the teachers as well as the pupils were big into their football and you were an instant hero, I loved all the attention.

I played for the Croydon district team as a left midfielder. Life was good, but then dad retired from boxing, took on the Park Tavern pub in Streatham and we moved to live there.

It was a disastrous move for all of us.

~ PARENTS AT WAR ~

The screams were piercing. The shouting was intense.

I was at the pub with Rebecca. My mum and dad had been having more and more arguments, but this one was worse, much worse. Me and my little sister looked on as dad had his hands pressed firmly around mum's neck. He was strangling her and she was in pain.

Now my dad was no woman beater so this was a shock. He was a womaniser though and moving to the pub seemed to make him worse.

Boxers, like a lot of footballers, often went into the pub trade when they retired from competitive sport.

I was 9 or 10 at the time. It was a bad move for everyone, as this is where my mum and dad started having their differences.

Dad was a bit lost as he'd just finished his boxing career. I was to feel the same way, but worse, when my football career was coming to an end.

While mum worked hard (she basically ran the pub), my dad would wander about chatting to the punters, flirting with the ladies. Everyone knew he was this boxing champion and he commanded respect.

And he knew it and took advantage of it.

I knew what was going on and so did mum. She bottled it all up at first. Sure they'd row about it, but mum then had an affair of her own and dad had clearly found out.

My mum and dad were so wrapped up in their own circumstances me and Rebecca were now very scared.

I ran into the room begging dad to stop, I was crying my eyes out, Rebecca was as well. Luckily one of mum's lady friends, Kim, Tracey and Perry's mum, was there and we managed to break it up.

That was the end though. There was no going back for my parents. I found their wavering commitment to each other hard to cope with. My understanding of marriage became confused and I have no doubt in my mind that what I saw with my parents affected the way I behaved with women later in life.

It's not an excuse for some of the stuff I did, but it is an explanation. Weakness where women are concerned is a sort of addiction and it had been passed down a generation to me.

~ BULLIES ~

I changed school to one called St Leonards and I hated every minute of it. I was bullied, particularly by a big black kid called Dennis.

Kids knew I was the son of a boxer, but that seemed to make them more determined to test me. Dennis came after me most days.

I was an easy-going youngster who made friends easily, but Dennis didn't take to me at all and he picked on me relentlessly. He didn't like the fact that I was popular for a start.

I must have had a fight every day at that school and I wasn't winning many of them. Life was sad and I received no backing from the teachers.

The head teacher was a right bitch who just had no time for me at all. She was happy just to brush every problem under the carpet and hope it would go away.

My parents' problems with each other were not helping either. I remember getting beaten up one day and ringing my mum begging her to come and get me. Now I love my mum with all my heart, but I hated her that day. She came to school but refused to take me home. She basically told me she wanted to help, but she couldn't take me there and then.

She was immersed in her own troubles and couldn't help me with mine. I was left at the school gate dying inside.

I wanted someone to put an arm round me and help me, but my own mother and my head teacher didn't want to know.

I was getting bullied and I had to resolve the problem myself. It was kill or be killed so to speak.

Dad had a gym in the pub and I was like Rocky's son in Rocky 5, the one played by Stallone's own son Sage. He also had to learn to fight to survive.

I put on some gloves and started working out. I knew straight away that some of my dad's ability had rubbed off on me. I was only 9, not particularly big, but I discovered I could punch.

I'd been training for a couple of weeks non-stop when Dennis came for me again. I remember him shoving me against a wall getting ready to pummel me.

But this time I fought back. Bam! I smacked him with a right hook and split his lip. He had massive lips and blood was shooting out from them.

It was a great shot. He burst into tears and even though I got punished for it, and my parents were called in to receive a complaint about my behaviour, it was worth it because Dennis was more careful with me after that.

Dad was pleased as he'd always told me to defend myself. He knew kids challenged me to fights because of who my dad was so it was vital that I could fight back, even against kids much bigger than me.

He nodded politely at the head mistress who ticked me off, but he was chuffed for me inside.

I really believe I could have been a boxer, a very good one. I was actually more passionate about fighting than football when I was very young, but I just knew I had a chance of making the grade at football and that sport wouldn't hurt so much!

Becoming a professional footballer was one of my recurring dreams as I loved the thought of scoring goals in big games.

My father and I had discussed trying for the Olympics as a boxer or for me to continue my journey at Crystal Palace to go on to be the best footballer I could be and to be fair I never looked back once I'd signed my YTS at Selhurst Park.

My dad would have loved me to box, but he respected my decision and he still backs me in everything I do.

~ CHILD ABUSE ~

Also at the pub I was abused. At the time it didn't seem that big a deal, but I realise now I should have reported it.

Instead I didn't tell a soul.

I was a 10 year-old boy taken to bed by a 25 year-old woman. I didn't feel degraded, I actually felt quite excited, but I now know that this woman must have had serious issues and God only knows what she got up to later in life.

The Park Tavern was a big pub and we used to take in lodgers. Lots of them.

One night, mum put me to bed, but I was soon woken by a tall, blonde lady who appeared at my door. She was attractive and she beckoned me to go with her.

I was a kid, I had my pyjamas on for God's sake. What on earth was she thinking?

But I was used to doing what adults told me to do. She took me into her room and we chilled for a bit on her bed before she told me to get under the covers with her.

She started touching me and told me to touch her. She made me do things to her that I had never done before. I won't lie, it wasn't horrible, but I wonder to this day whether or not that night was to have an effect on me in my later years.

To this day I haven't told anyone. I realised at the time that she was doing something bad, but she was also being very nice to me and as a result I didn't want to get her into trouble.

She left the pub a few days later. The experience was a bit beyond my understanding given the age I was.

Nowadays it would be treated as abuse and I wish I had said something.

~ DAD ON THE WARPATH ~

Mum eventually left dad and took us with her. We went back to Thornton Heath which was cool for me apart from one fact – she moved her boyfriend in with us.

He was an Irish guy called Joe and I had no time for him. He couldn't replace my dad in any way, shape or form so we didn't get on from the start.

It wasn't the end of the family fights either. Dad beat up this guy a couple of times and one time I had to stop him actually killing him.

Me and Joe clashed constantly. He had no idea how to treat a child and to be honest he didn't try that hard.

On one occasion, he was just waffling on about some shit in the sitting room. He tried to get me to tidy up, but I refused so he chucked a ball at me. I chucked it back and shouted that I may be small but I'd fight him.

He wanted to take me up on the offer so I legged it upstairs and rang my dad. 'You're dead' I told Joe as I ran out of the room. Little did I realise I might actually be right.

I told dad what had happened. He lived 20 minutes away, but 10 minutes later I looked out of my bedroom window and saw this huge man with a black angry face running down the road.

I had never seen him like that and he must have flown as he arrived in our street so quickly. This meant trouble, for Joe. I hated that man, but I regretted the phone call.

I shot down the stairs, went out the door and told dad everything was cool. Mum came out, but Joe cowered inside, probably crapping himself with good reason.

If dad had got through that door there would have been a murder. Joe liked a drink and he probably wet himself that night.

I don't want to waste any more words on him now. He had issues that caused him problems later in life.

Mum did split from him eventually, but that night I made my mind up to move on again. I was 12.

I told mum that I needed to live with dad. I needed a proper father figure to guide me in my life.

It broke my mum's heart. I loved her. I told her that, but the day I left she sat on my bed sobbing.

I didn't know it then, but I left one 'interesting' household to live in another.

Dad was living well now. He was in Coulsdon and he was boxing professionally again making good money when I moved back in, but he had a girlfriend with him. She was 17, not much older than me.

I thought it was pathetic that a man like my dad had a partner just a few years older than his oldest child.

She was just too young to do 'mummy' things, but to be fair she tried and she was with my dad for 10 years, giving him two children Christopher and Alexandra, my brother and sister.

It's funny how I did the same thing as this woman, as I was behaving as a father at the age of 17.

I found out she'd met my dad in the pub. She was one of his many girlfriends from that time.

~ GOAL MACHINE ~

They were weird times for me, but football became my release. I was now at Woodcote High school which was a good school.

I was a popular pupil, especially with the ladies. Being good at sport helped with that and I revelled in the attention.

I loved people watching me perform. I had a certain way of moving on the pitch that attracted attention.

By the time I was in the fourth year (15) at Woodcote I was essentially running the school. I was bossing it because of my sporting prowess.

I'd turned into a confident kid. One day a young girl came up me, said 'are you Leon McKenzie?' and then asked me to sign her autograph book.

Soon there was a queue of kids asking for the same. I could see all the teachers watching and wondering what the hell was going on. I wasn't surprised though. I'd been practising my signature for months as I knew by then I was going to make it as a footballer!

I enjoyed Woodcote, but I also experienced racism from a kid called Coleman. He went as far as to threaten to stab me after school.

I called dad to tell him what had happened and he raced down to the school gates.

The whole school had heard about this potential fight and most had turned up to watch. I must admit I had some butterflies, but my dad turned up and I immediately felt a lot more relaxed.

My dad stepped out of his car and just said 'Is this him?' I nodded and he nodded back which suggested I should get on with the fight.

I went up to Coleman and landed several huge punches. I beat this kid up badly in front of teachers, parents and the other kids. They all knew what Coleman was like and I earned a lot of respect that night.

Mr Staley was my football teacher at Woodcote and he started playing me as a striker. For the first time in my career, I was a forward and I took to it straight away.

At this time, I was introduced to Chipstead FC. I couldn't stop scoring for school and club, I started to realise I might have a future in this game.

And that was just as well as I wasn't good academically. I was a joker with a feisty side. I was good at English, great at drama, but rubbish at maths (I cried my way out of the top set and into the bottom set with the other numpties where I was much happier).

I was hopeless at exams. I'd be coming to the end of page one when the other kids were finishing.

I came out of school with GCSEs in English, Drama and PE, but nothing else. I effectively finished school at 15.

For a while, reality hit me. There was no way my pride would let me sign on the dole so I needed a job, a trade, but I also had the number of Peter Nicholas, the Crystal Palace youth team boss up my sleeve.

I rang Peter and begged for a trial and my hunger must have been obvious as he agreed.

CHAPTER 14

'FATHER'S PRIDE'

Leon's father is Clinton McKenzie, a three-time British light-welterweight boxing champion, who now runs his own gym in Dulwich.

Clinton was the eldest of seven children born in Jamaica who emigrated to England when he was nine years old.

Clinton won the British Light-welterweight title three times, but possibly his most famous fight arrived in his amateur days.

Clinton boxed for Great Britain the Montreal Olympics in 1976 and in the third round he had to face the great hope from the United States, one Sugar Ray Leonard.

Leonard won the fight on a unanimous decision (he won all his fights on unanimous decisions on his way to the gold medal), but Clinton impressed onlookers with his courage, as well as his ability, after taking a standing eight count in the second round.

Clinton turned professional the following year and finished with a record of 36 wins (12 by knockout) and 14 losses in a 50-fight career that lasted 12 years.

But ask him what makes him more proud than any of his own successes and the answer will involve his own eldest son Leon (Clinton has six children in total by four different partners).

Clinton's always been there for his son whether it was on the touchline as a schoolboy football career started to flourish or at the end of a phone when Leon needed to hear a friendly voice.

Most dramatically Clinton saved his eldest son's life when Leon believed suicide was the only solution to severe mental problems. Clinton recalled: "Nothing can prepare a parent for the sight of seeing their child close to death. I know that I wasn't ready for it and I pray that no other parent has to see what I witnessed.

"When I burst into that hotel room in the middle of the night I was shocked, appalled even and most definitely frightened.

"Leon, my eldest son, and a man who had brought me so much happiness and generated so much pride in me was lying on his bed. He was barely conscious and he certainly didn't know where he was.

"He was completely out of it. He mumbled a few incoherent things, but nothing that made sense. It was a race against time to save him.

"Instinct does take over in situations like this. We tried to keep him awake while we waited for the ambulance. We just about managed that, but we still travelled to the hospital terrified about what the final outcome would be.

"I had picked up the phone to Leon at midnight or 1am, or sometime in the middle of the night anyway, and listened for what seemed like ages to my son pouring his heart out to me.

"He was always an emotional, sensitive child. He was tough on the outside, but inside he cared deeply about those close to him.

"I'd had many chats with him about life in general and sometimes he was a bit down, but on this occasion he sounded in desperate trouble.

"He kept repeating 'I've had enough dad, I've had enough. I can't cope with life anymore.' It didn't register straight away what he was planning and what he was trying to tell me, but then he muttered something about taking lots of pills so I knew I had to get to him as quickly as possible.

"He was alone and he was stumbling over his words, but I made him tell me where he was and I shot round there at 100 miles an hour. Luckily I wasn't too far away and the traffic was light.

"I got to him in the nick of time. The ambulance was there soon after and he made it to hospital where they told us a few more minutes or a few more pills and Leon would have been gone.

"It was traumatic seeing him in such a bad way. Leon had always been a handsome, energetic, athletic boy and he had turned into a top-class sportsman so to witness him in such a pitiful state was heartbreaking for all the family.

"I'd rounded all the family up and got them to the hospital where we spent a nervous night. When we realised he was out of danger we knew we had to rally round and keep his spirits up.

"But having seen him that night and the following night, and seeing him now, I have to say I am more proud of Leon now than ever before.

"The way he has turned his life around has been heroic. He was at death's door and although he was saved, it takes a special kind of man to recover from being that low.

"As a family, we have always been there for him, but his recovery is really down to his own determination and fighting spirit.

"He's not just stumbling along either. He's not just getting by. He's given himself challenges, dreams and targets for the future which he is busy fulfilling.

"I'm proud of Leon for what he achieved in football, but the way he is now using his problems and his experiences to help others is truly inspiring.

"I think Leon would have been forgiven for going into his shell after all that has happened to him from the suicide bid to the stay in prison, but instead of hiding he has been very open about his life, warts and all.

"The reaction of the public to a high-profile footballer admitting to weaknesses has been very positive and long may it continue.

"We have had our ups and downs like all families. We had a family tragedy that pulled us apart well before Leon's troubles, but we are all very close now.

"I've always been proud of all my kids, but the first-born is special and Leon was truly a gift from God.

"That's what I said when he was born. That day was the proudest of my life and Leon has never done anything to change that opinion.

"He could be a cheeky and boisterous child, but he gave us a lot of joy as parents and showed us a lot of love.

"My passion was always boxing and I did think that Leon would follow in my footsteps and those of his Uncle Duke by becoming a professional fighter.

"I have no doubts that he would have been good enough. Leon had so much natural talent I believe he would have succeeded in any sport he chose to take up.

"I remember a newspaper coming round to the house when I was preparing for a fight. They wanted to take some pictures of me play-boxing with Leon, but Leon started hitting me so hard I had to get him to stop.

"He was five at the time!

"I also remember when I was playing the role of the 'Comeback King' as I prepared to fight Lloyd Christie in Birmingham.

"I was trying to win the British title for the third time. It was a big deal at the time as boxing, even for British title bouts, was very high profile, but I felt terrible on the day of the fight.

"I'd split up with Leon's mum by then and I was feeling miserable. There was no way I could win in that frame of mind.

"But an hour before we were due to climb into the ring, the dressing room door swung open and there he was.

"Leon's mum had let him come up to Birmingham. He'd been dressed up to the nines and his obvious joy at seeing me gave me a lift.

"We embraced and I knew from that moment that there was no way I could lose. I went on to deliver one of the performances of my life to win on points and that was down to Leon as much as me.

"Leon was really good at judo and athletics as well as boxing, but he decided he had a chance of becoming a professional footballer and I was never going to stand in his way. I wouldn't have been able to even if I'd wanted to as Leon has always been very much his own man.

"Like most devoted dads I stood on the sidelines watching him bang in goal after goal for whatever club or school team he was playing for and it was soon obvious that he had a gift.

"The day he signed a youth team contract at Crystal Palace was a great day for our family and then when he made his debut for the first-team it was even better.

"Watching this local kid, my son, come out of the tunnel with the other first-team stars was impressive enough, but then he scored in the last minute and picked up the man-of-the-match award and all his family and friends were pinching themselves to make sure this was really happening.

"Me, Leon and his granddad were invited to meet the first-team manager Steve Coppell in his office the following day and when he offered my son his first professional contract there was a tear in my eye.

"He was so happy back then. Palace was our club and Leon was Lord of the Manor. He went to Wembley with them as a teenager and although he didn't get on, it was still a memorable occasion for the family.

"I was blown away by my boy and although he had to take a step back to Peterborough to get his career moving forward again I just knew he would make it back to the top again.

"He seemed to be popular wherever he played. The Peterborough fans loved him as he scored regularly and gave his all in every game for them.

"He grew to love that club, but Barry Fry was always telling him he was destined for bigger and better things.

"He was a hero at Norwich when there was a time when he seemed to score in every game and to see him in the Premier League playing against the likes of Manchester United and Chelsea, well that was just incredible.

"He had issues with his divorce while at Norwich and I knew that the injuries he had at Coventry were starting to get him down, but I had no idea that he was suffering from depression.

"I knew he got down at times, but then who didn't?

"Leon hid it well from us because he didn't want to burden us with his problems. I feel very sad when I look back at those times. I often try and think if there was any way that I could have helped.

"The suicide attempt was obviously the time when Leon reached the very bottom and the way he has turned his life around since then is nothing short of miraculous, especially when you think of the trouble he's been forced to get through since.

"My son is not a bad man and he's certainly not a criminal so to see him sent to prison for a few speeding offences was distressing.

"Leon wouldn't let me visit him in prison even though I would have gone over there at the drop of a hat. That was his way of coping and I respected his wishes.

"I was sure he would cope with whatever prison slung at him. By the time he was sent down he was dedicating himself to his lovely family and he had set out in pursuit of other dreams.

"When Leon focuses on something I know he will make it work. I told him to make prison work for him. It was important he made the most of whatever was thrown at him.

"He can never give up on life again, because you don't get another chance.

"But when he went inside he was already a different man to the one I found in that hospital bed so I was confident he would come through it okay.

"And he has. Leon is now so strong mentally I would back him to do well in whatever he chose to do.

"I'm happy he's now decided to take on boxing and I'm proud to be helping him along with my brother Duke.

"Leon is 34, but he's not a novice at the sport. He's been in the gym since he was 10 years old working out so he already knows the basics.

"He knows how to fight now so if we can teach him the other necessities he can win a few fights.

"Leon isn't stupid and I wouldn't think British or European titles are on his mind, but boxing is in his blood and I think he needs to prove that he can perform in the ring.

"The Prizefighter series on Sky is his target. He could win one of those and retire happy that he has proved that he can fight like a McKenzie!

"He has nothing to prove to me though. He's already my Champ."

CHAPTER 15

'HIGHS AND LOWS'

I wish I'd played a few more seasons in the Premier League as the better the standard, the better I played.

I never really felt I could make it to international football, certainly not with England, but you never know if I'd managed to stay in the Premier League I could have become a late developer like Darren Bent and forced my way in.

Obviously, I would have loved to have played for my country. I can't imagine what that would have felt like, but I made the most of what I had and I am proud of that.

I remember watching Michael Owen's famous World Cup goal for England against Argentina and feeling so excited and happy for him. I had played against him in youth football and it was only a couple of years later that he was performing on the biggest stage of all.

I can't kid myself though. He was on a different planet ability-wise to me.

But I also felt my body would let me down in the end so when I was playing in the Premier League I never felt I had a serious shot at going higher.

I did qualify to play for Jamaica through my father, but although I went over there to train with the national team I picked up an injury and never really tried again.

I achieved something 90% of players didn't and that was playing in the Premier League so I could hardly complain.

And considering the number of injuries I had I played an amazing number of matches. Too many were as a substitute, but I passed the 100 goal barrier which was one of my targets.

I made the best of the ability I had. I never gave less than 100 per cent in any game even though there were times when my mind was more willing than my body.

Obviously, I retain a great affection for Crystal Palace. I had to work hard to get my foot in the door, but to play for my local team and to score on my debut was just amazing.

I was a Palace supporter before I played for them and Ian Wright and Mark Bright were my heroes.

It's a shame it ended badly thanks to Alan Smith, but I played in the Premier League at the age of 18 and I will always be grateful to Palace for that.

I didn't want to move permanently to Peterborough. I enjoyed two loan spells there, but they were only ever designed to enhance my chances of getting into the Palace first team.

But leaving Palace and dropping down a division proved a blessing in disguise, at Peterborough I was top man, the star of the show and guaranteed to play in the first team.

I scored regularly and played well. Manager Barry Fry was superb with me and if anyone was going to get me back closer to the big-time it was him.

Peterborough was good for me and I was good for them. I had some personal difficulties in my time there, but the club were never anything less than supportive.

I spent three good years at London Road and I had a special relationship with the fans. I thank everyone connected to the club for what they did for me.

Peterborough was the only club that I didn't leave under a cloud! My days at Norwich City were simply the best in my playing career. I played my best football and played with some great players.

Scoring twice on my debut against the 'scum' helped, but the fans at Carrow Road were always behind me and the team.

Thanks to Norwich I played at Old Trafford, Stamford Bridge and St James' Park. Thanks to Norwich I competed against Wayne Rooney, Cristiano Ronaldo and a host of other top-class players.

It didn't end well for me at Norwich either, but there was too much going on in my life off the field and I had no choice but to leave.

Norwich manager Nigel Worthington and chairman Delia Smith were great with me though. They knew about my personal issues and tried their best to help me.

If I could have made decisions purely based on football I would never have left Norwich.

I had good times alongside the frustrating times at Coventry, but I felt they treated me badly towards the end of my time there.

Coventry is a fantastic club who play in a fantastic stadium. They didn't see the best of me as I played a lot in midfield for them rather than in my best position up front.

The change of position may have been one reason why I started picking up so many injuries. My body was having to do different things and my knee was reacting badly, while I was also collecting a lot of muscle injuries which was new to me.

I thank Mickey Adams for making me a million pound footballer and I was sad to see him leave even though we had to do far too much running in training under him!

Coventry had good coaches as well in Frank Bunn and Alan Cork. Cork had terrible banter, but he was the perfect coach for a striker and I have a lot of respect for him.

Scoring my 100th goal was one of the highlights of my professional career and that happened at Coventry so there were some good memories from my time at the Ricoh.

I received plenty of messages along the lines of 'I enjoyed watching you play', from Coventry fans when I left, which was in keeping with the messages I received from most of the fans of the clubs I represented.

Unfortunately, I was becoming increasingly worried about the future when I was struggling at Coventry and the attitude of chairman Ray Ranson seemed uncaring and unsympathetic.

My biggest regret was not showing Charlton what I could do. I feel guilty that I spent almost an entire season injured.

I tried to commit suicide during my short spell at the Valley, but that wasn't their fault. The blame for that lay with the injuries I couldn't shake off and the fact that my career was rushing to its end.

I honestly feel that a player joining Charlton now with the symptoms of depression that I was showing would be looked after.

There is so much more awareness now and a failure to help me in my time of trouble was a football issue rather than a club one.

My spell at Northampton was fine at the start and only ruined by the arrival of manager Gary Johnson.

Northampton signed me knowing I was having trouble in my personal life and when the prospect of prison was hanging over me, but while one manager Ian Sampson was there for me, Johnson, on the other hand, in my opinion couldn't care less.

I'd never played for a club who struggled as much as Northampton did when I was there and most of that was down to Johnson.

Johnson and Smith were by far the two worst managers I ever encountered. Coppell was the best.

Even Kettering Town provided me with some 'interesting' memories and I'm now playing for Corby Town in the Blue Square Conference North Division.

My old Northampton manager Sampson took me to Corby, but he's already gone and Chris Plummer is now in charge.

Sampson met me by chance one day when we were both golfing at Collingtree Park. I was well and truly retired by then, but Sampson was very persuasive and it was a fact that he had been good enough to send a character statement to the court ahead of my sentencing.

He also flattered me by saying how fit I was looking!

The money wasn't going to be great, but I went along to training. It was quite a good little stadium, they seemed a good bunch of lads so I thought sod it I'll give it a go.

I signed a non-contract deal which meant either party could terminate the arrangement with seven days notice.

We were flying in pre-season, but we lost our first five league matches and Sampson left after a disagreement with the chairman.

I must admit at that time I was close to quitting for the second time in a year. I didn't want to be losing in the Blue Square North Division every week, while getting into verbal spats with some meathead defenders who saw dumping me on the floor as something as a scalp.

I'd remind them that I was now 34 and that I've had my career in the Premier League. Playing against Corby is as good as it's ever going to get for you so don't try the verbals on me!

As much as I still loved football, I wasn't enjoying the results and I was disappointed for Sampson when he left because we hadn't performed for him. I rang him and apologised for what had happened, but he just told me to keep going.

Chris Plummer took over straight away and that saved me. He has Mark Peters as his coach and Ian 'Minty' Jackson as his goalkeeping coach and they are all quality people.

Chris has been good to me. He realises my body won't let me play every game so I want to repay him with some good performances and goals when I can.

He likes what I bring to the team in terms of guiding the younger players and I have enjoyed the experience a lot more in recent months. Even when I only get on for 20 minutes at a time I believe I am still making a contribution.

We have ex-Northampton defender Jason Crowe in our team so we have quality and we get crowds of between 500 and 600, not that many, but their vocal support is always guaranteed.

I've scored a few times, but I won't deny it's hard for me. We only train twice a week and I usually only get to one of the sessions!

It was never about the money for me. I just wanted to play professionally so I'm proud to have made over 400 appearances. I'd have been happy to play 10 games so 400 is just phenomenal. Reaching 100 goals was a massive milestone for me, although it was a shame that the 100th came against Norwich!

I hope the Norwich fans have forgiven me for that and I want to thank the supporters at Palace, Peterborough, Norwich, Coventry and Northampton for their backing throughout my career.

I know they realise it just wasn't about scoring goals for me. I gave 100 per cent in every single game and no player can do more than that.

I set out at every club to win over the fans and that meant playing hard in every game even those with little meaning at the end of a season.

I hope I will be remembered for that as much as for any goals I scored.

~ CAREER STATS ~

(Appearance total is inclusive of substitute appearances, although sub appearances appear in brackets)

CLUB	FROM	TO	FEE	APP. (SUB)	GOALS
Crystal Palace	1995	200	Trainee	98 (47)	8
Fulham	1997	1997	Loan	3 (2)	0
Peterborough	1998	1998	Loan	15 (0)	9
Peterborough	2000	2003	£25,000	103 (8)	49
Norwich	2003	2006	£325,000	81 (32)	22
Coventry	2006	2009	£1 million	68 (21)	14
Charlton	2009	2010	Free	14 (14)	1
Northampton	2010	2011	Free	27 (10)	10
Kettering	2011	2011	Free	9 (3)	2
TOTAL			**£1,350,000**	**418 (137)**	**115**

*Leon has never been sent off in a professional career that is in its 18th year.

~ SEASON BY SEASON ~

SEASON	CLUB	APPEARANCES (ALL COMPS)	GOALS
1995-1996	Crystal Palace	12	1
1996-1997	Crystal Palace	24	2
1997-1998	Crystal Palace/ Fulham	7	0
1998-1999	Peterborough/ Crystal Palace	31	10
1999-2000	Crystal Palace	26	4
2000-2001	Crystal Palace/ Peterborough	45	13
2001-2002	Peterborough	35	20
2002-2003	Peterborough	11	5
2003-2004	Peterborough/ Norwich	41	20
2004-2005	Norwich	37	7
2005-2006	Norwich	21	5
2006-2007	Norwich/ Coventry	38	9
2007-2008	Coventry	11	2
2008-2009	Coventry	23	4
2009-2010	Coventry/ Charlton	20	1
2010-2011	Northampton	27	10
2011-2012	Kettering	9	2

~ MONEY AND ME ~

I never earned more than £10,000 per week.

I was on £250 at Palace at the start which went up to £1,200 before I left for Peterborough. Peterborough paid me around £1,500 a week at the start which rose to £1,800 before I left.

Norwich doubled that to £3,600, but that went up to £7,000 per week when we won promotion to the Premier League.

I had goal bonuses and appearance money in my contract which pushed me up to an average of £10,000 per week, but never any more.

Coventry took that salary on when I moved there. I was on £9,000 a week with them which was slashed to £2,500 before I moved to Charlton for £3,500 per week.

Northampton paid me around £900 per week, but I'm not sure what I was on at Kettering as they didn't always pay me!

I do wish I'd managed my money better. I must have spent £100,000 changing cars every year.

I've owned three Mercedes, three Range Rovers and a Porsche Cayenne in my time. None of which I really needed and their ownership was more a case of keeping up appearances.

I didn't gamble heavily, but I did become addicted for a while to roulette in Casinos. I won £17,000 one night in Vegas playing the game and lost £22,000 the following night.

Betting shops had no appeal to me, although I did play with a few footballers who had serious addictions and would bet on anything.

I was permanently close to being bankrupt. I've had multiple warnings, letters and visits from bailiffs, but I'm coping much better now. There are debts, some big ones, but they are under control.

I've suffered because of a couple of bad property deals when I trusted people I shouldn't have trusted, and my own generosity as well as a stupidly expensive divorce.

I would never turn down a plea for help when I was earning well and some of the people I lent large amounts of cash to have never paid me back.

One such person I will name. He is Michael, aka Melody, who was involved in the hit song 'do you really like it'.

We became friends about seven years ago. He came to my stag do and to my wedding. I was warned not to trust him by my friends who didn't really like him, but I just felt he was a lost soul who I could help.

He used to think he was a bad boy, but he was all talk. He came to me one time when he was about to lose his pad at Chelsea.

He was crying down the phone so I lent him thousands of pounds to save it. He went on to lose the flat anyway so it was already money down the drain and when I asked when he was going to repay me he just fobbed me off.

I stayed patient, but a year passed and he manufactured an argument when we were doing some music together and I am convinced it was deliberate so to give him an excuse to avoid me and not to repay me.

I've never had a penny back from him or even an apology. We haven't spoken in years and I don't expect to ever again.

People let you down in life and you live and learn. I now have the people I need around me.

~ GREEK TRAGEDY ~

Before I signed for Northampton I went over to Greece and had a trial with Kerkyra FC. They played in the Greek top flight and they were keen to take me on.

They offered good money, but I was hearing so much about players getting paid late or not enough or not at all that I turned them down.

That scenario was bad enough for a club on my doorstep. I wasn't going to travel a few thousand miles for the same thing to happen. Then there was the racism....

I don't have any regrets about my career. My main aim was to play in the Premier League and I got there twice.

I've had some career threatening injuries but I still had a successful 16 year career which is something I take with me.

My first major injury was aged 21 when I was playing for Palace v Huddersfield. I had three operations as a result, but I still managed to make a decent career.

That was thanks a lot to Steve Coppell who let me rest during the week, train on Fridays and then play on Saturdays. Without that considerate management I might not have lasted as long as I did! I'd say injuries in the end defined how far I would go. I ended up having eight major operations in 14 years as a professional.

Who knows where I would have ended up if I'd have managed to stay completely fit.

Having said that though I also owe my private physio David West and Erol Umut (aka Turkish, who was also a pupil at Woodcote School when he had a big afro), Peter Webb, who was Erol's assistant at Charlton, plus the physios at my clubs Paul Showler, Neil Reynolds, Stuart Barker and Michael McBride for keeping me in one piece.

~ LEON'S HIGHLIGHTS ~

The best games, goals and players from Leon's career.

~ BEST MATCHES ~

1

Saturday, April 9, 2005
Premier League
Norwich 2, Manchester United 0
Attendance: 25,522.

The best side Norwich ever beat. Few gave us a chance, but we harried and harassed them for 90 minutes and deserved a victory that is still talked about in Norwich now.

Dean Ashton opened the scoring and I scored a second 10

minutes later. Just a perfect day and a result that gave us hope that we could beat the drop.

United brought three reasonable substitutes on, but we were not going to be denied that day.

Norwich: Green, Helveg, Fleming, Drury, Shackell, Stuart, Safri, Francis, Huckerby, McKenzie, Ashton. Subs used: Bentley, Jonson, Svensson.

Manchester United: Howard, G. Neville, Ferdinand, Heinze, Silvestre, Kleberson, Scholes, Smith, P. Neville, Fortune, Saha. Subs used: Rooney, Van NIstlerooy, Ronaldo.

2

Tuesday, October 3, 1995.
League Cup First Round Replay.
Crystal Palace 2, Southend 0.
Attendance: 6,765.

My debut at the age of 17 for my hometown team has to be up there as one of the greatest experiences of my life.

And I would have said that even if I hadn't scored the match-clinching goal. To feel the love of the Palace crowd who got behind me from my first kick of the ball was the most beautiful feeling.

Jamie Vincent opened the scoring and I added the second goal in front of all my family and friends. Life doesn't get much better than that.

Crystal Palace: Martin, Vincent, Gordon, Shaw, Coleman, Roberts, Houghton, Southgate, Pitcher, Dyer, McKenzie.

3

Sunday, December 21, 2003.
Division One
Ipswich 0, Norwich 2.
Attendance: 30,152.

What a way to introduce yourself to a new club! Two goals on my debut against the local rivals in a game that was shown live on national television was just an amazing experience.

Manager Nigel Worthington took a gamble in throwing me straight into the game, but I repaid him with a goal in each half.

They were life-changing goals for me and proof that I responded best when put under pressure to perform.

It was the perfect way to start a journey which ended with promotion to the Premier League a few months later.

Norwich: Green, Edworthy, Mackay, Fleming, Drury, Henderson, Mulryne, Holt, McVeigh, McKenzie, Svensson. Subs used: Roberts, Jarvis, Brennan.

Ipswich: Davis, Wilnis, McGreal, Santos, Richards, Wright, Magilton, Bart-Williams, Westlake, Bent, Kuqi. Subs used: Naylor, Counago, Mahon.

4

January 22, 2005.
Premier League
Norwich 4, Middlesbrough 4.
Attendance: 24,547.

This was a game that summed up that season in the Premier League for us. We played well, but let in daft goals and relied on a great never-say-die attitude to get us a point.

I was a sub and when I came on after an hour we were 3-1 down. It was soon 4-1, but incredibly we scored three times in the last 10 minutes to get a point.

Dean Ashton started the comeback, I made it 4-3 in the 89th

minute and then left-back Adam Drury of all people popped up with an injury-time equaliser.

Damien Francis had opened the scoring for us, but two goals from Jimmy Floyd Hasselbaink and two from Franck Queudre looked to have sealed the win for Boro.

It was just an amazing game to play in and we felt like we'd won the league when we came off the pitch.

Norwich: Green, Edworthy, Doherty, Brennan, Fleming, Drury, Mulryne, Francis, Huckerby, Jonson, Ashton. Subs used: Holt, McKenzie, McVeigh.

Middlesbrough: Schwarzer, McMahon, Reiziger, Queudre, Southgate, Doriva, Parlour, Zenden, Downing, Desire-Job, Hasselbaink. Subs used: Morrison, Graham.

5

Tuesday, April 10, 1996
FA Youth Cup Semi-final First Leg.
Liverpool 3, Crystal Palace 1.
Attendance: unknown.

This was memorable because I saw at first-hand the amazing talents of Michael Owen. He was only 16, but he scored a hat-trick in both legs of the semi-final.

My first glimpse of him was frightening. He scored early on, I equalised with a lob, but Owen went on to run us ragged and claim a hat-trick.

I had a sense that I was watching a player who would become one of England's all-time great players and I wasn't wrong.

There must have been over 10,000 fans at Anfield that night and the Liverpool team also included Jamie Carragher.

Just to emphasise how good he was, Owen scored another hat-trick in the second leg at Anfield in a 4-4 draw. I was injured and missed that game, but I watched in awe from the sidelines, realising how far behind the very best players I was.

Line-ups not available.

6

Saturday, February 7, 2009
Championship
Coventry 2, Wolves 1
Attendance: 21,167.

Wolves were pushing for promotion when they came to the Ricoh and it was a competitive derby.

We were well up for it. We didn't want them celebrating on our patch.

Michael Doyle put us ahead in the first half, but they looked like getting a point when Sam Vokes equalised late on.

But three minutes later Jordan Henderson played a superb ball though for me and I dinked it over the goalkeeper.

The ball seemed to take an age to roll over the line, but our crowd went mad when the goal was given.

I was taken off a couple of minutes later and two weeks later I was injured and didn't play again all season.

Coventry: Westwood, Wright, McPake, Fox, Turner, Henderson, Beuzelin, Bell, Doyle, McKenzie, Morrison. Subs used: Best, Eastwood.

Wolves: Hennessey, Foley, Ward, Stearman, Berra, Jarvis, Henry, Kightly, Quashie, Ebanks-Blake, Iwelumo. Subs used: Reid, Vokes, Edwards.

~ GOALS ~

1

Saturday, April 9, 2005
For Norwich City v Manchester United (home)

Wayne Rooney lost possession to Youssef Safri who fed Darren Huckerby who passed to Dean Ashton and I just knew his cross would land perfectly for me to volley home.

I never tire of talking about that goal, the most special of my life. It just sealed my belief that I could play at Premier League level.

2

Sunday, December 21, 2003
For Norwich City v Ipswich (away)

The goal wasn't that great as I smacked the ball into the net from close range following a cross from Paul McVeigh, but the significance was huge.

It was my debut at my new club, it was on television, it was against our local rivals and the win sent us to the top of Division One.

3

Sunday, December 21, 2003
For Norwich City v Ipswich (away)

Many defenders didn't realise I was actually pretty good in the air as I proved here by rising above the Ipswich back four to head home Gary Holt's cross.

The goal sealed a 2-0 win and set us on the road to promotion to the Premier League.

4

Saturday, October 23, 2004.
For Norwich v Everton (home)

I scored my first Premier League goal in this game and it was all the sweeter as it was scored against my former team-mate, and Crystal Palace legend, Nigel Martyn.

I chased a hopeful ball forward, but used my strength and speed to see off David Weir and shoot past Martyn.

I could easily have gone down and won a penalty, but I was desperate to score and not certain to take the spot-kick!

5

Tuesday, November 10,198
For Peterborough v Cambridge United

When I went to play for Peterborough in the Third Division on loan from Crystal Palace, I was surprised how good some of my new team-mates were.

Midfielder Simon Davies was one of them and it was his pass that sent me through on goal in a big local derby match.

I was never going to miss and remembering that goal now still gives me a buzz.

~ BEST OPPONENTS ~

1

Thierry Henry (Arsenal)

The best striker I have ever been on a pitch with. He was big, rapid and so very cool!

When Norwich played against him, we were like little schoolkids trying to get the ball off the biggest and best player in the playground.

Arsenal beat us 4-1 twice in our Premier League season. He scored once at Carrow Road, but grabbed a hat-trick at their place.

2

Paul Scholes (Manchester United)

He was the greatest passer of the ball I have ever seen and he's still at it now in the Premier League which is just amazing.

It was an honour to get on the same field as someone like Scholes.

3
Ryan Giggs (Manchester United)

Giggs was brilliant when I played against him eight years ago and he's still pretty good now.
The ball was tied to his feet when he dribbled, even at the extreme pace he used to manage.

4
Xabi Alonso (Liverpool)

I watched in awe of Alonso when Liverpool trimmed Norwich up at Anfield. He oozed presence and I don't think he gave the ball away once in a passing master-class.

5
Michael Owen (Liverpool)

I only played against Michael once when he was 16 in an FA Youth Cup semi-final, but he left an impression on me that remains today.
We all knew then that this was a player going to the very top with club and country. His pace was electric, but his movement and finishing were also top drawer.
I thought I was a good player when I was teenager, but Michael was on a totally different level.
It's a shame that all his injuries caught up with him because if he'd kept his pace for all of his career he would have been unstoppable.

~ LEON'S ALL-STAR XIs ~

(Players he played with, and he insisted on including himself)
Nigel Martyn
Marc Edworthy, Richard Shaw, Gareth Southgate, Ashley Cole
Attillio Lombardo, Jimmy Bullard, Simon Davies, Darren Huckerby.
Dean Ashton, Leon McKenzie.
Subs: Matthew Etherington, Matt Jansen, Adam Drury, Clinton Morrison, Damien Francis, Bruce Dyer, Paul McVeigh, Dougie Freedman.

(Players he played against)
Petr Cech
Micah Richards, Rio Ferdinand, Ledley King, Ashley Cole.
Cristiano Ronaldo, Paul Scholes, Steven Gerrard.
Denis Bergkamp Thierry Henry, Craig Bellamy
Subs: Frank Lampard, Jermaine Defoe, William Gallas, Ryan Giggs, Alan Shearer, Xabi Alonso, Theo Walcott.

~ BEST GROUNDS ~

1
Anfield

There's something about this place that gives you goose bumps. Lining up before the start in the tunnel and watching all the Liverpool players touch the 'This is Anfield' sign is quite unnerving, but also quite touching.
I loved playing there and scoring at the Kop End in that youth team cup tie was a very special moment. Liverpool always had great fans who got right behind their team.

2
Old Trafford

There were 67,000 people there the night I came on as a substitute to play against Manchester United for Norwich in the Premier League.

It's just an awesome feeling playing on that pitch in front of packed stands that reach up to the sky.

3
City of Manchester Stadium

I played badly there, but that didn't spoil the enjoyment of seeing this impressive stadium for the first time.

4
Ricoh Arena

I didn't have the best of times at Coventry, but I had a couple of special moments at the Ricoh Arena.

It was a modern building and when the Coventry fans were in good voice, as they were when I scored in a big game against Wolves, the place just rocked.

5
Carrow Road

My debut for Norwich City was perfect apart from one fact. I just wish I'd scored two goals against Ipswich at home rather than away.

But I loved playing at Carrow Road. They were my happiest days in football so the home ground itself will always be special for me. It was the best football of my life against the best players, the best teams and in the best league in the world.

No Highbury, White Hart Lane or Stamford Bridge in my list as I just didn't think they were that special in terms of atmosphere or in the stadia themselves.

CHAPTER 16

'FUTURE DREAMS'

I throw my heart and soul into everything I do. No matter what I take up I want to become as good at it as it's possible to be. When footballers retire from the game, they need challenges to keep themselves in shape physically and mentally.

When I'm 60 I want to look back at my life and be able to say that I had a bloody good go at everything I took up and that I have no regrets.

I could have made a comfortable living as a footballer in Leagues One and Two, but I wanted to do better than that. I wanted to be as good as I could be and that meant playing in the Premier League.

Life is about following your heart. You should ignore the negative people who put doubts in your mind by saying you'll never make it at something.

In fact, you should use them as motivation. You should want to prove them wrong and that's what drives me on.

Boxing is my new focus right now and I want to have a real go at becoming a professional. Boxing has obviously always been in my blood. I'm a McKenzie after all.

It would make me so proud to get the McKenzie name back in the headlines in that particular sport.

I've been sparring and working in gyms virtually all my life and once I have my boxing licence and I have passed a medical I will be signed up as a professional and I'll be trained by my dad and Uncle Duke.

They both have some fantastic training methods which will complement each other perfectly. It can only help that I have such pedigree in my training camp and I hope Duke will be in the corner with my dad when we start fighting.

Duke's a bit reluctant to be in my corner at fights as he's not sure he wants to be too close up when someone he loves so dearly is in action. I hope to persuade him as I look up to him so much and having him close by will inspire me.

I trained with a former European champion Spencer Oliver while I was preparing for the fight game.

I took Spencer's breath away when he first saw me in the ring at his gym in Finchley. He reckons I'm a natural and he is adamant I will have a decent career even though I'm 34 already. Spencer will also have an input into my career.

I like to think I was a thinking footballer. I could do quite clever things on the pitch and it's the same in the boxing ring.

I must admit the thrill of knocking an opponent out with a single punch probably would match scoring against Manchester United in the Premier League, but I'm also fascinated by the art and science involved in boxing.

My dad was a brainy boxer as well as a hard man and I reckon I will fight just like him. Duke was a special technician so between them they should be able to help produce a decent fighter.

I'm very confident I can make it a fair way. I may be a rookie professional, but I've had the skills drilled into me from an early age and I'm unbeaten in fights against bullies, racists and footballers don't forget!

I already understand the basics. I know how to stand and I know how to move and with a bit of fine tuning I know I will win a few fights.

I need to train hard though. I've already started the training runs at 4.30am so the drive is clearly there.

I'm out early in the morning three times a week. I'm in the gym three times a week as well.

I want to take part in one of those Prizefighter nights on Sky which boast a first prize of about £32,000.

That's my first goal. I reckon I could hold my own at super middleweight. I'm an avid watcher of boxing on the television and I'm sure I could be as good as some of those guys once I've stepped my training up.

I should generate a bit of attention as a footballer taking up a new sport, a bit like Curtis Woodhouse did when he made a similar move and now he's an English champion which is a great achievement after a dozen or a so fights and shows what can be done with the right level of dedication.

I wouldn't fight Curtis though as he's too small!

I've already appeared on Sky television's Ringside programme so my dream is out there and I'm confident I will succeed.

I can't leave any questions unanswered. It's a brutal sport, but I have people I can talk to about what's required.

My Dad and Uncle Duke will be involved in my training and having a British Champion and a World Champion in my corner can't do any harm.

I loved watching the pair of them fight. The atmospheres and the occasions used to give me a real buzz and I can't wait to step into ring and feel the same.

I will go in front of the British Boxing Board of control soon to get my boxing licence and once I have that I have to pass a medical. If I pass that then I hope to fight for the first time in February at York Hall in Bethnal Green.

That's where my dad made his professional debut which makes it an even better story. He was made up when I told him the plan.

I know I could sell tickets with the right promotion and ideally I want to have three fights before I'm 35 in May and then I'll step on to the big stage.

I'm just ticking over in the gym at the moment, but once I have a definite fight date I will be at it 24/7.

Sadly, if my boxing takes off I may have to scale down my football commitments at a time when I am enjoying the crack at Corby.

I may have to ask the chairman and the manager for some unpaid time off to concentrate on my boxing as I don't want to run the risk of injury halting my new career before it has started.

My other passion is singing, but any career in music will have to wait until the boxing has stopped.

I've been a performer from a very young age. I have always enjoyed showing off to a crowd.

Between the ages of 7-10 I attended Gloria Berry's drama school in South London with my sisters Rebecca and Tracey, and Tracey's brother Perry. One of my fellow students was Nicola Stapleton who went on to play Mandy Salter in EastEnders.

I had parts in the 'King and I' and 'Carousel' and I loved it. I was acting rather than singing, but people used to tell me I had a decent voice when they overheard me singing along to my favourite records.

I loved music in the 1990s. Michael Jackson, Marvin Gaye and Bobby Brown were particular favourites of mine. I saw Michael Jackson live in concert at Wembley and it blew me away.

Obviously football got in the way so any thoughts about a music career were put to the back of my mind, but it has always been part of my life. The right song has always been able to inspire me, just like Whitney Houton's song did when I was in prison.

I did cut a record though when I was at Peterborough with a friend. DJ Spoony is a long-time mate of mine so he managed to play the record on Radio One which was an incredible buzz, I was just 23 at the time.

I felt I was good, but I was better at football so I could only drift in and out of the music scene.

It was a good way of getting away from the pressures of professional football, but later in my career it was an even better way of getting away from the madness in my mind.

I used to go to the studio after training just to take my mind off my problems, but I was just dabbling in it then.

I will be committing to it at some stage though. I've performed a few times in front of an audience including one at the Brickhouse in London and another in Peterborough and it has gone superbly. It doesn't quite deliver the excitement of playing top level football and scoring a goal, but maybe one day it will.

I'd love to have one hit record. That would satisfy me and I have some great people around me to help me make it happen.

I wrote a song 'Finally' which Harvey and Lady Leshurr performed with me. That went down well on itunes with the public as there were about 30,000 pre-orders of the song which is a pleasing number.

The song is doing okay, but me going to prison at the time of the song's release affected the sales. I was in prison so I couldn't promote the song so my excitement and enthusiasm was dampened, so please buy it now to make up for the lost time ha ha!

It took me four hours to produce the melody and the verse. When I have words going around in my head I find it quite easy to get them down on paper in the form of lyrics.

But obviously Harvey helped me a lot as well.

We've been friends for a long time and I'm blessed to have him as a friend. He looked up to me when we were both young footballers and I obviously look up to him as a musician.

Harvey wouldn't have put his reputation on the line if he didn't think a song like 'Finally' could work. I've been working with producers in London for a few years now so I have the contacts in place should the singing ever take off. They have made encouraging noises about my voice so I'm very positive about making it work.

I have other songs ready and waiting for release. I am releasing an EP called 'Give it to me' (featuring my boy Doom Man, a top lyricist) and soon after the new year I will releasing an R & B EP, which is my favourite genre, my true musical love.

Music came into my life at a time I needed it. I can't live without it. I'm an R & B singer really, although I'm pretty open when it comes to musical tastes. I do like Ne-Yo and I love Marvin Gaye's style and vibe, while I can perform acoustic songs as well.

I've appeared in a few of my own videos which is also cool.

There is a bit of musical talent in my family. Most of my cousins are very talented. Jermaine is pretty good.

I'd love to perform live at a music festival. I've coped with crowds of 50,000 in my football career so I'm sure a big music crowd wouldn't bother me. In fact it's more likely to inspire me as I thrive when my adrenaline is pumping.

Not many people who dream of being a footballer make it into the Premier League and not many people who dream of becoming a singer manage to make and sell a record, but for my singing this is only a start.

I'm not necessarily out to become more famous. If that happens then so be it, but I want to be recognised and perhaps acknowledged in the music world, if only for making music that people enjoy.

I certainly don't see myself as a top artist and I'm not looking to compete with the real top professionals, but if I can give pleasure to some people through my singing then that will make me very happy.

You can have more than one dream in your life. Turning those dreams into reality is a fantastic feeling.

It can never be a case that when your first career ends then it's the end of your life.

I don't want to be one of those people who just spend their time chatting shit on the internet rubbishing the efforts of others who are still trying to achieve things in their life.

I want to be out there trying to succeed again. I have a saying that I carry around with me that explains my motivation.

It reads:

'When I stand before God at the end of my life, I would hope not to have a single bit of talent left so I could say I used everything you gave me.'

CHAPTER 17

'DON'T GO DOWN MY PATH'

I'm now working for and helping a new company called Elite Welfare Management (EWM).

EWM is offering support and education to professional footballers who are struggling with their lives in any way shape or form.

We have people on board like me whose own experiences can be used to help others in similar situations and we hope to work alongside other organisations that have player welfare on their agenda.

We hope to receive some financial backing from the Professional Footballers Association (PFA) and we also had a recent meeting with the Sporting Chance clinic which was very positive.

Hopefully, we can all work together to address a problem that has been neglected in the past.

I am the living proof of what can happen to footballers who are not prepared for the end of their careers.

EWM believes prevention is more important than the cure so part of my role will be to educate players to spot the signs of depression, anxiety and stress etc and to be able to deal with it by seeking expert help from the likes of me.

The death of Gary Speed brought the world's gaze onto depression within football and to me it's obvious that this is an area that the

PFA, who are a very rich organisation, should become involved in financially.

I stayed silent after my own suicide attempt which was very wrong. Thank God I have had no relapses, but I was scared inside for a very long time.

In my opinion players should know they have someone to talk to about their problems no matter how serious they are or how embarrassing they think they are.

I didn't have that luxury, but it's a situation that has to change. I discovered that bottling your emotions up does you no good at all.

I have spoken to Mickey Bennett of the PFA on several occasions and asked how I could get involved with them, and how I could help players facing the issues that are so serious today and that so nearly killed me.

Now the PFA do some positive things and they say they have been working in these areas for some time.

They claim that only since Speed's death have others tried to get involved in a more high profile way.

That's untrue in my case as I had been lobbying the PFA before then. I admit it took Speed's sad situation to make me speak out publicly about my suicide and my depression, but the PFA will hopefully note how well received my actions were.

EWM met with John Bramhall of the PFA and he is to talk about the possibility of funding our enterprise with chief executive Gordon Taylor which is an encouraging sign.

When I first approached the PFA, I was told to go away and do some research and to come back when I had a plan.

This is how I came to join up with Vincent Pericard (a former Stoke and Portsmouth player) and John Duncan (a psychology professional) at EWM.

These people had the same visions, the same ideas as me and I will be getting some professional training in psychology which combined with my own personal experiences will hopefully make me an even greater help to fellow sufferers.

I am to be called a foundation consultant and I'm going on courses which will help me give the best possible advice to sufferers in the best possible manner.

I believe I'm already a good listener and I interact well with people. It's a role I am determined to make a success of, with or without the help of the PFA.

We intend to travel to meet footballers who need help or they can come to us.

We've had several wonderful meetings at EWM and we have a fantastic retreat at Capesthorne Hall in Cheshire.

It's a place where we can put on educational programmes and counselling programmes to help the mind.

I've spoken to many players since my own suicide attempt mostly because they approached me out of concern for their own situations.

Trust is a key issue here and players clearly trusted me as I was one of them, a professional footballer who has had a lot of issues with depression.

And, crucially, I come out the other side in good health, in good spirits and in a good frame of mind.

When I mentioned the EWM project to these players, they were all for it. They would all have been happy to come to me and other members of the group for guidance.

It was a no-brainer for me, but our original meeting with the PFA didn't go well.

I believed them when they said that they received proposals like this all the time and it would be naive to expect the PFA to fund everything that is placed in front of them, but they should have been more open and honest with their plans.

Basically, the PFA left the meeting with an open mind, but with no guarantees of help at that time, which was actually a massive disappointment to us. Our opinion was that if they don't want to put money into something that is so blatantly needed then they should have been brave enough to say so.

There should have been no beating about the bush and no

attempt to say something just to placate us. That was just wasting everyone's time.

At EWM, we didn't want to be in the position where we are forever chasing the PFA for answers, but we left the meeting totally confused.

In my entire professional career I paid my subscription into the PFA. From the age of 17 I was contributing and I want to be taken seriously when I speak about other people who have suffered like I have.

I retired from the game feeling so lost and empty I needed support. Yet I never had a phone call from the PFA to ask if I was okay. I never had a phone call from the PFA asking if there was anything they could do for me.

It wouldn't have taken a lot for someone to call and say: "Leon we are sorry to hear about your attempted suicide, but if you need any help please call."

I tempted sufferers out of the woodwork. The first step on the road to recovery is often admitting and confronting your problems and I have seen evidence of that from the players who contacted me after I went public.

The PFA issued a booklet on handling depression a couple of seasons ago. It was 36 pages long and was sent to all 4,000 current full-time professional footballers before Speed's death and 50,000 ex-players after it.

It appears that the PFA were the ones that actually became more active after Speed's death.

The advice was good, but is sending out a 36-page booklet with a few helpline numbers on it enough? I don't think so as so much more could have been done.

I suspect the PFA know that now. That's why they decided to act so publicly when a high-profile former player, whose actions attracted attention all around the world, was lost.

My own view is that the PFA shouldn't have waited until Speed passed away. They should have acted on the phone calls people like me were making.

They were genuine warnings from genuine people. We were also scared that many other players were facing deep problems.

Speed wasn't the only high-profile suicide case. German goalkeeper Robert Enke was at the peak of his career when he took his own life aged 32.

I'm sure I wasn't alone in making such calls. In fact I know I wasn't, but it took a high profile case to make the PFA go public.

I believe the PFA is too political internally and it saddens me because it is so obvious, from talking to its employees, that certain people within the organisation do not understand depression at all.

Mickey Bennett is not one of them, but this is too much to put onto one person.

As time goes, on I'm sure they will be trying to understand and I hope that we can find the common ground so we can push on together.

I see the PFA at the centre of our business. They invest a lot of money into other areas so why not an area that would effectively save lives?

Why does there have to be a guarantee that if they put £500,000 into something they get it back as soon as the business does well as was suggested?

Some things are more important than money and mental health issues are at the very top of that list.

A booklet that goes out to families is all well and good, but knowing that you played a part in saving families some serious heartache must surely be more rewarding in the long run?

I really hope the PFA will back us in the serious areas that need to be addressed. It would have been better to have said at that original meeting: "look we can't give you anything yet, but if it develops well come back to us."

I guess you have to understand depression first before being able to listen.

At least now we are getting somewhere and the PFA are now starting to listen and there are more positive signs that there will be support given.

There is nothing more disheartening than seeing people who can help, walk away from proposals that mean a lot to you, but the level of co-operation we are receiving is now sitting nicely with me.

I'm sure the PFA have helped some players, but they work at their own pace, to their own time scale and in future cases they may well be too late.

I am an individual who has suffered and all I want to do is be part of something that helps players weather their own storms.

I hope to see more understanding towards what EWM are trying to achieve. Sitting at a desk as a businessman discussing figures is okay, but there has to be some education of the illness. If you don't understand the seriousness of depression you won't be so emotionally attached to the project.

Once you appreciate the seriousness of the illness, you are more likely to support it.

Now that's great, but the problems with professional footballers, even those at the top of the game, go a lot deeper than just sending them to a place like Sporting Chance.

Players with mental health issues need regular inter-action and a caring attitude. I accept the need for a business to make money, but players with depression need trust that the personal touch provides.

Whatever happens, I am committed to helping as much as I can through EWM. It's a project I really believe in.

Statistically, one in 10 people suffer from depression at some point in their lives and one in 20 people are in a battle with clinical or severe depression.

If there are 4,000 professional footballers that's 400 who have dealt with or are dealing with depression.

If there are 50,000 ex-players, as the distribution of the PFA booklet suggests, that's an astonishing 5,000 sufferers.

Yet how many examples of footballers with mental health issues do we hear about? Nowhere near that many and they are the people that EWM wants to reach out to and help.

Mental health is being talked about more and more and not just in football. Golfer Paul Lawrie talked about his bouts of depression before the Ryder Cup recently so public awareness is being raised.

Ideally we will get to footballers before illness drags them down. We are aware of many situations that can bring a player down like long-term injuries, re-location and we can educate players in all of that as well as helping to manage their ambitions. I have players and ex-players reaching out to me all the time. I tell them to focus on what's ahead and how rewarding it can be just to see your life get back on track. I know this from personal experience. It's an opportunity that I'm passionate about and I just hope we can make it work.

CHAPTER 18

'ANGELS'

My own suicide bid was selfish.

Eight years earlier I'd been on the other side of suicide when a friend, who was so close to me I referred to her as my sister, took her own life.

To understand depression you have to learn about depression. I didn't know much about it then but I obviously have more of an understanding now.

Me and Tracey were inseparable. Our mums, Donna and Kim, were very close so it was natural that me, my biological sister Rebecca, Tracey and her brother Perry spent a lot of time together. Tracey was the naughty one in her family, and I was the cheeky one in our family. If anything went missing me and Tracey would be blamed which was okay as we were usually guilty.

We did nothing seriously bad and we certainly weren't malicious children, but we caused our parents no end of worry with the scrapes we'd get in to.

When dad had the pub, Tracey and I would go upstairs to make water bombs and throw them out of the window at the customers. Everyone knew it was us, but we had the charm to go with the cheek and we'd get away with most things.

We'd go to school together. We'd play together. We did everything together and that didn't change even throughout our teens. We had no secrets and we shared each other's joy and each other's pain.

She was made up for me when I started being successful at football.

We stayed close even when we had partners. Tracey had a three-year relationship which ended when she was 18/19. I'd be the person she turned to for support and I'd drop anything to go and be with her.

I was her big brother. I had had similar experiences and I just wanted to help her. I wanted her to be as happy as me.

She was beautiful and she owned the most massive, gorgeous smile which I can still see today.

Tracey had a few jobs, but none of them fulfilled her. I always told her she should have been a professional artist. She was fantastic at it. She wasn't thrilled with the actual jobs she had, but she seemed to be coping okay.

Then one day she telephoned me out of the blue. I was in Peterborough at the time. "Hi bruv," she started as normal, but the cheerfulness in her voice did not last long.

She went on to say how down she was, how hard she was finding her life.

Tracey was mixed race like me, but with lighter skin than mine. She said she was struggling to find her identity. She was single at the time living with her mum and her mum's partner, but she was struggling to fit in with her white friends or her black friends. Tracey had no satisfaction in her life from her work or her friends. She was alone and confused.

It was of course all in her head. Everyone who met Tracey loved and respected her. Everyone, family and friends looked forward to seeing her as they knew she brightened up any room she entered.

I don't know to this day what triggered her depression because it appeared so sudden to me. I was 100 miles away so I wasn't with her every minute of the day anymore – I was detached from her day-to-day experiences.

I could tell though from her tone of voice on the phone that day that she had issues, but I didn't realise how bad things were. I spoke at length with her and tried to be her big brother by telling her that she was a great person and that things would turn around for her.

I thought I'd said all the right things. I finished the conversation by promising to get back down to London to see her soon.

I wasn't just saying it either. I would go there as soon as I had a spare minute. That girl was as dear to me as my blood family.

I never had the opportunity. Two days later I was sitting in Peterborough United's car park waiting to go to training when my mum rang.

She was hysterical. She could barely speak, but she finally got the words out that crushed me; 'Tracey is dead son.'

Tracey had stayed the night before at her beloved nan's house. Her nan was on strong heart medication in the form of pills and Tracey had swallowed some.

They were powerful pills and Tracey soon realised what she had done. She tried to make herself sick by drinking some washing up liquid.

Her nan found her on the floor of the kitchen the next morning. She had passed away.

I was distraught. Thoughts were racing through my head, but few of them made any sense to me. One thought did keep recurring and that was what would have happened if I'd gone down there to see her as soon as she had called?

She took her own life just 48 hours after she rang me, but I could have saved her. We were so close she would have listened to me and I would have been able to calm her down.

Tracey was 23 and to this day I believe she was making a cry for help rather than trying to kill herself. To this day the incident makes me feel sick because of what I might have, should have, done.

I skipped training at Peterborough that day – as usual manager

Barry Fry was very understanding – and raced down to London.

As you'd expect, I arrived to witness dreadful scenes involving family and friends. An amazing, funny beautiful girl had gone from our lives and no-one could believe it, never mind understand why.

It was just a heart-breaking time for everyone who knew her.

When I turned up to her house in Mitcham, Kim saw me and burst into tears and ran upstairs. My heart sank going into the house as it just brought back all my memories of Tracey and the good times we had together.

I still find it so hard to go to Kim's house because of those memories. I can feel Tracey's presence and that is so upsetting, but I go and visit Kim and Perry whenever I can.

The funeral was tough on everyone. I broke down when the coffin was carried in. The saving grace was the hundreds of people who turned up to pay tribute to her.

It was a fantastic gathering of all the people who were touched by this beautiful, loving young woman.

In quiet moments, I still say a little prayer for Tracey. I once celebrated a goal for Peterborough by showing off a T shirt with her picture on it.

I didn't understand why anyone contemplated suicide. It was beyond my comprehension then, but because of what I've been through myself since, I fully understand it now.

There are a variety of reasons why depression strikes, but there are also many symptoms that can be picked up by those with a good knowledge of mental illness.

I know them all now. I didn't know them at the time Tracey needed help.

Victims of depression are sad all the time, they feel helpless, they feel guilty, they feel worthless, they lack motivation, they are indecisive, they become irritable quickly, they get no enjoyment out of life, they have anxiety attacks, they can't sleep despite feeling listless all the time and of course in the most severe cases they turn to suicide.

They also withdraw from their social circle including their family and closest friends. I recognise virtually every symptom from my own experiences, but 10 years ago depression was not as widely discussed in public as it is now.

If it was, Tracey could have been saved. As it was, I still feel I could have saved my sister.

Tracey remains my angel and she's joined in heaven by someone else who was very dear to me.

My mum's dad Frederick used to come and watch every game I played. He was a special person in my life and someone I could talk to about everything and anything.

Fred used to help train boxer Frank Bruno in the early days of his career. It was through him that my mum met my dad.

I was always close to him. He was always available with words of encouragement at any stage in my life, and it made me feel a million dollars that he was so obviously proud of me.

Fred came to Crystal Palace matches and he came to the games at Peterborough even after he'd been diagnosed with bowel cancer. He ignored his own troubles to continue supporting his family, particularly me. He was always positive and told me not to worry about dropping down the Football League to join Peterborough because he was convinced I would soon be spotted by the bigger clubs if I scored goals regularly.

Fred was adamant I had the ability to play in the Premier League and his confidence rubbed off on me.

Sadly, the cancer finally condemned Fred to hospital and it was tough for all of us to see him in pain during his last days, time he spent in ghastly circumstances in Mayday Hospital, the place where I was born.

That hospital was disgusting. To see a 60-something year old man treated with such indifference as he waited to die was just horrible, but I at least made sure he took a lovely thought with him as he passed away.

I was at Peterborough at the time and it was rumoured that Glenn Hoddle wanted to take me to Spurs. I knew the interest was genuine as I'd heard it from sources I trusted.

I also knew that Peterborough manager Barry Fry asked for too much money so the move never happened.

But one of the last sentences I uttered to Fred was: 'Granddad I love you and I'm going to Spurs for £1 million'.

The words brought a smile to his face, but within minutes he was gone.

When I'm feeling down now, I always reflect on Fred's pride in me and in what I had achieved.

He supported me in everything I did and although he wasn't around when I got back to the Premier League, I just know he was looking down on me with a massive smile on his face.

CHAPTER 19

'NEAREST AND DEAREST'

Throughout my life, I've been lucky to be loved and supported by some fantastic people. There are family and friends who have been with me every step of the way, who have never judged me or reproached for what I've done, and who will never be forgotten by me.

Sometimes they have said harsh words to me, but they have acted in my interests all the time. I'm so grateful for their love.

First and foremost is my beautiful wife Sofia, my Queen B, my rock.

If you've ever seen the Rocky films, you'll know what I mean when I call Sofia my 'Adrienne'. Adrienne was the wife of Sylvester Stallone in Rocky and she steadfastly supported her man no matter what scrapes he got into.

We've had our situations, our issues and she has stood by me through some awful times when lesser women would have cut and run.

She loved me through my suicide bid and throughout the police investigation and prison. She never once wavered and I will be eternally grateful.

We met in London where the Norwich players were having a Christmas party. Sofia was with friends and I spotted her when she walked in. This was a vision of beauty and I was smitten.

When she started dancing I went over to her straight away, flirting, doing my thing, but she was not in the slightest bit interested. Instead she was playing it cool.

Paul McVeigh, a shorter, less good-looking Norwich team-mate, decided to try his luck. 'Listen mate,' I said. 'If she's not interested in me she certainly won't be interested in you.'

Sofia laughed, 'Macca' didn't. It had broken the ice. She said later that she found me attractive, but the humour had won her over. She got one of her friends to give me her number at the end of the night.

I called her, and decided to tell her straight away about my personal situation. I was married to Vanessa but in the process of completing a divorce at the time.

I told her I was playing at Chelsea that Saturday, which was close to where she lived, and if she came to watch me play I'd take her out afterwards.

Now Sofia knew I was a footballer, but she didn't know to what level so when she realised I meant playing at Stamford Bridge and not some local park, she was a bit dubious about meeting me.

Anyway after the match I drove round to her house as arranged. It looked like no-one was at home. The lights were all off. She came out eventually and admitted she'd thought about cancelling right up until the last minute as she wasn't sure she wanted to date a big-time footballer.

Footballers didn't have the best reputation with the ladies, but I assured her I was different and thankfully she believed me. We went to an Italian restaurant and we hit it off straight away.

I was impressed that she clearly didn't just want to the girlfriend of a footballer. She was interested in me as a person.

I was still attracting women in Norwich at the time, but I knew Sofia was the one when I was taking a girl called Anna home, she straddled me in the car as soon as we got back to her house.

Normally, I wouldn't need a second invitation for something like that, but something had changed inside of me. I had feelings for

Sofia, I didn't want anyone else.

I made my excuses and left.

Sofia loves me in a way that I can't explain. She is not interested in money, she is interested in me and she believes in marriage which is just as well for me. She just gets the whole 'for better or for worse' part of the marriage vows.

She has had plenty of reason to leave me but she won't. Marriage to her is a special thing, a bond between two people who love each other that can't be broken.

I owe her my life. She has accepted some of the derogatory things I have done and helped me put things right.

Sofia has a degree and she has her own business. She does not see me as a provider. We have created two beautiful daughters.

There have been times in our relationship when I have abused her trust and taken her for granted, but she realises that depression clouds your judgement and disturbs your vision.

She understands and accepts that I lost myself for a while.

I'm running out of lives though. I need this strong, fantastic woman by my side. Luckily for me she feels the same way.

Sofia was involved in one of the most nerve-wracking moments of my life though. Believe it or not I became quite the traditionalist when it was time to propose and I decided to formally ask her father's permission to marry his daughter.

We flew to Spain. I took a big photo of me and Dean Ashton celebrating a Norwich goal, gave it to Sofia's father with words written on it in Spanish asking if I could marry his daughter.

There was an awkward silence which seemed to drag on for ever, but actually lasted about 20 seconds before he said yes.

I won his respect just by asking, never mind in such an unconventional way.

My children saved my life and now they are my life. They and Sofia are the reasons I am determined to make a go of my second chance.

My son Kasey, my first-born, is a fantastic kid, but he's still searching for his identity which we all do at that age. I am carrying on the family tradition by calling him 'Champ' and I'm sure he will earn the title!

Kasey looks up to me as someone who has achieved fame and recognition and I'm sure it will have a positive effect on his life as he turns into a man himself. He will understand success is not all about fame and money, and he will hopefully learn from the mistakes I have made in my life.

My champ believes he has to match my success or he will be judged a failure. That is certainly not the case as far as I am concerned and we've spoken many times about the subject.

As long as he puts his heart and soul into whatever he chooses to do then I will be happy. He can drive a bus or stack shelves in Tesco, it doesn't matter to me as long as he does his best, is respectful to those he works with and that he always provides for his own family.

Fame and money is cool if it comes along, but it doesn't arrive for most people so life should be about finding happiness for yourself. The rewards will come later. I'm very proud of my son.

My dad was a British Boxing Champion, my Uncle was a boxing World Champion, but they never put me under any pressure to succeed. When I found football they were thrilled, but they had supported me and guided me rather than pushed me and I will be the same with my children.

I'll be their dad no matter what happens to them. I can guide them through my own experiences. One of my favourite quotes comes from Michael Jordan and I've instilled it into my son: 'I can accept failure, but I won't accept not trying.'

Everyone fails sometimes. I messed up exams at school all the time and I've been knocked down several times in adult life, but I have always managed to bounce back and that's the sort of character I want to instil in my own children.

As kids lots of things will be difficult to understand. Only as we get older and become adults do things become clearer.

My children have seen my trials and tribulations, they've seen me go in and come out of hospitals and they've seen the interviews

I've given recently about depression and suicide, but the love they've shown me has been unconditional.

There's only one way I could ever be sent back to prison and that's if someone harms my kids. If anyone ever tests me in that way I will be using my skills like Liam Nielson in the film 'Taken'! My daughters Mariya (9), my princess, Naima (4), my sweetpea, and Talia (2), baby T, are so precious to me and I'm so proud to be their daddy. I hope they will be proud of me as they grow up.

When they tell me they love me, which they do all the time, life makes sense again.

I still have 'down' times when I think of what I would have put them through had I left them behind as I'd once intended.

Thank goodness I failed. I have got myself through a lot of personal shit with no professional help, but there is no doubt that Sofia and my four children have helped me achieve this just by being themselves.

My kids are my world now. Everything I do from now on I do for them as well as me. The younger ones keep me positive just by coming into my room and jumping on my bed to cuddle me.

That makes me get up and battle on and appreciate the blessings I have in my life.

The simple pleasures are the best pleasures.

My babies gave me the will to continue and I gain strength from them. When I see their faces, the way they smile, the way they kiss me, the way they look, to see the love they have for me no matter what, it's just an inspiration.

The thought of leaving them behind as I so nearly did stays with me every day. Their presence has made me get hold of my mind and forced me to change the thought patterns that so nearly killed me.

God has really blessed me with such amazing and beautiful children and I thank my ex-wife Vanessa and Sofia for them.

My parents Clinton and Donna are astonishing people. Sure they had their ups and downs when together, but my mum and dad gave me a happy childhood and their support in the bad times has been just phenomenal.

I love them both very much. I also feel very close to them.

I'm very protective of my mummy Donna. She held down two or three jobs at a time to help to raise me and my sister Rebecca in a comfortable fashion.

There was a time when we grew apart. She moved to Canterbury with that prick Joe and I resented that for a few years.

If I'd had my mum around I wouldn't have made duff decisions like moving in with Vanessa when I was too young.

I would have popped round to see her and I'm sure she would have talked me out of the stupid stuff, but as far as I was concerned Canterbury was on the other side of the country and I didn't make the effort to see her.

I still feel guilty about that, but we are over it now.

Grandad Fred's death made me realise I needed my mum and I reached out to her again. We've been close ever since and I'd damage anyone who harmed her.

Happily she's now married to a top bloke called Brian who will be her third, and final, husband! Mum still works ridiculously hard as there isn't a lot of money about in the family, but she does it to make sure all her children, she has five, are safe and secure.

When my finances were in better order I bought her a horse as she loved riding. I also bought her a designer watch which reduced her to tears as she said no-one had ever bought her a present like that.

I was glad to do it. It made me happy as well because she was forever putting others above herself. If I had looked after my money better, my mum would not be working now, she would be going on holidays abroad twice a year and enjoying life. Maybe I will get to that stage again.

On the day of my suicide attempt I rang my mum from outside the hotel. I could hardly breathe. I was having a panic attack and I told her I couldn't take any more. The injuries were hastening the end of my career and I'd had enough.

She burst into tears and begged me to give up football because of what it was doing to me. She hadn't quite taken in what I was about to do and that was my intention as I was serious and I didn't want her to even try and talk me out if it.

That was selfish of me and when I woke up in hospital and expressed disappointment that I was still alive, she stormed out of the room.

She couldn't believe I could say something so disgusting and, again, selfish. I wasn't well and I wasn't thinking straight as I can now see the devastation it would cause if your children passed away before you.

I realise how bad to everyone I loved I was at the time. I put them through some horrible times, but my mum has stayed strong and the fact that all her children love her to pieces proves she has been a big success in life.

My Dad, Clinton, is quite simply my hero. It's important for children to see their parents do something so positive and my dad showed that natural ability is not enough on its own to succeed, you need dedication as well.

I used to see my dad come home from the early morning training runs all boxers have to endure to reach the top dripping with sweat, but he never missed one. He would be out there pounding the streets come rain or shine, and it was mostly rain as I remember.

Dad was a grafter and there's no question that I wouldn't have achieved what I did in football without the benefit of his guidance, expertise and love.

He conducted himself in a thoroughly professional manner at all times. Sure he'd let his hair down when he was between bouts, but when a fight was approaching he would get himself into the best possible shape to give himself the best chance of victory.

He's 57 now and that dedication is still there. He still works out at his gym and he still shows passion and enthusiasm to all his clients.

His life is his gym now. I'm excited that he will be helping me with my boxing training and I know he will get a kick out of it as well.

He knows that I will give it my all, or he wouldn't get involved. I'm not looking at what he or Duke achieved, I'm looking at what I can achieve. For me just to step in the ring as a professional after the career I've had in football will be an incredible feeling.

I saw my dad's dedication from a young age and I used to go out on extra training runs when I was a young footballer at Palace as a result of that. I went from being one of the average players in the youth squad to the best because dad had passed his work ethic down to me. He taught me to go out and earn what I considered my right.

Dad also saved my life. I rang him after I'd taken the pills, not because it was a cry for help, but because I wanted to speak to him one last time.

For all I knew he could have been on the other side of the country, but he happened to be close to the hotel, less than half an hour away and he burst into the hotel room in the nick of time.

I did think the last thing I would see was my dad's face because I thought I had died, but as it happens he saved me. I wasn't pleased at the time, but I am enjoying my new life and my family because of him.

Dad was naturally shocked at what I had tried to do, but he showed me love and compassion. We speak every other day now and we are very close.

Dad also passed down some not-so-good habits like messing around with women, but I never judged him on that.

He's with a woman called Clare now who, to me, is not good for him or our family.

Dad has six children by four different women, but to me he's just a very special man with strong values and deep down I know he has an awful lot of love for his family.

I sometimes feel sad as dad should be in a better position financially after all he achieved in boxing, but his heart, desire and pride is worth fortunes and I'm proud to able to call him my dad.

My sister Rebecca is like a twin. She always said she knew when I was in pain and that used to hurt her.

Rebecca is a very emotional person and when I was sent to prison she became hysterical as she wasn't sure I'd be able to cope.

She sent me beautiful letters straight from the heart while I was inside which I obviously appreciated.

She cares deeply for me. She remains a wonderful sister.

I also have a sister Alex who is very beautiful. She has two children of her own with her husband Zak who is in the army.

If ever I go to London I usually stay with her family. We have a really good relationship and I'd do anything for her. I'm very proud of her.

Christopher is another brother. He has started an amateur boxing career and he's doing well, having lost just once so far.

He's very reserved, but as he gets older he's gaining confidence and I speak to him often on a one-to-one basis to offer guidance. He's not much older than Kasey so I can relate to him in a brotherly way.

Since splitting up my mum and dad, with their partners, have given me other brothers and sisters .

Natalie, who has just had a baby, is another lovely sister of mine. I love her and even though we don't speak a lot, my home is always open to her.

It's the same with Aaron, another brother who lives with my mum in Kent. As a big brother, if ever he need's me, I am here for him.

Lauren is another sister who I love very much.

Casiyah is a sister who lives in Scotland. When I was in Coventry I met her for the first time when she was about nine or ten.

It was awkward for us both, but as a big brother I felt I had to meet her. She is around Kasey's age, but we haven't spoken for a while and I hope that changes soon.

I've always looked up to my uncle Duke McKenzie and not just because he was a three-time world boxing champion and an MBE.

He has always treated me like a son. He's been through a lot himself in life and he's worn the 'T' shirt of life, but he's always been there for me with advice and guidance.

Duke spoke up for me in court and laid part of his own life bare in the process, just in an attempt to help me.

He also spoke at my wedding and bigged my boxing prowess up which was good of him! He's also going to help me train so I'll be a rookie with a World Champion and a British champion in my corner.

Duke came to the hotel the day after my suicide attempt and he was in tears. We sat together for three hours and cried a lot during that time.

He told me about all the personal things he'd been through and how he fought his way through them. It was an inspiring few hours and it definitely helped me get my life back on track.

When your back is to the wall you realise who cares for you. I am so lucky and so grateful that so many people look out for me.

I definitely need Duke in my corner with my dad.

Damien McKenzie is my cousin. He's seven years younger than me, but we pretty much grew up together.

My dad was doing well financially when I was a kid and we'd have the families round to our big house for barbeques and stuff when we'd have reggae music blaring out in the garden all day and night.

Damien's dad was Ray, one of my dad's six brothers. His mum was Pauline who was an awesome, beautiful woman whom I had many talks with and I often stayed round her house as back then I was close to Damien's brother Omar (Damien being a bit younger than me).

Ray was for me a waste of time and the way he has treated Damien and Jermaine is the reason why I have no respect for him because they are like brothers to me.

Me and Damien used to lark about as kids. We lost touch a bit when I moved to Peterborough, but we became close again when Pauline passed away.

Her last words to me were to ask me to look after her boys and I hope she's satisfied with how I've fulfilled her last wish.

I've tried to be there for them whenever they've needed my help and I believe Damien must have been grateful because he really stepped up when I started hitting problems.

He'd seen me mess up, but he's never shown me anything other than love and respect. He was another one to stand by myside throughout the worst of times and I'm so proud of how he has turned out himself.

He's a teacher and he's engaged to another teacher, Michelle who I am happy to say will soon become a McKenzie.

Michelle is a very intelligent girl, fantastic at art in particular. We have little jokes about Manny Pacquiao and Floyd Mayweather. She is from the Philippines and whenever I visit the house is always full of her relatives as they are a very close knit family I call them the 'Pacman' family.

Damien wrote me a letter while I was in prison which was incredibly touching.

Me, Damien and a lad called Daniel formed a bit of a 'wolf pack' with me as leader of course. We could visit the worst places imaginable and still have a great laugh.

I got to know Daniel through Damien and we became close mainly through going out and making pests of ourselves, well more so Daniel but when all 3 of us are together we always get so much jokes without fail. Daniel has a good heart and is someone I see as close friend, I'm looking forward to Damien's wedding, I can see a (Hang Over Part 3)!

Jermaine was also a great lad. He loved his music and he founded the Team McKenzie clothing range.

Jermaine also wrote to me when I was in prison as did another cousin Duke who I don't see that often, so it was especially good to hear from him when I was inside.

Duke was also into his music. I am proud to be part of a very talented family.

My boxing connections helped me to meet Nigel Benn, a great British world Boxing Champion of the past.

He invited me and my family to stay at his house a few years ago. He's a legendary boxer who used to love beating people up in the ring, but he has transformed his life outside of sport and he did his bit to set me on the right path again after I had tried to commit suicide.

He was quite hard on me, but he was doing it for the very best of reasons. I failed him because I was still very lost, but he got through to me by opening up and revealing his own battles against the strains he was suffering.

He reckoned he saw something of himself in me and he opened up to me about the problems he experienced during his career.

He didn't have to show me such kindness, but it did open my own eyes and he has helped set me back on track now.

I thank him and his wife Caroline for the love they showed me and my family.

Kimberley is another cousin whom I love very much. She is forever checking on me and she wrote to me regularly when I was at my lowest.

I don't see her a lot, but she has passed all her lawyer exams. It's a shame she didn't pass them a few years earlier as she might have kept me out of jail!

Michael Duberry is a great friend from the world of professional football. What he did for me and for my family while I was in prison means I will always be in his debt.

We first met when I was with Vanessa and he was with an ex-girlfriend. We had played against each other, but never socialised until the last few years and we quickly became close.

When I was in prison he would contact Sofia regularly to make sure she was coping. He's a big man, but a gentle soul and he watched over the family as I'd asked him to and he showed her that she was not alone in a difficult situation.

He'd also make sure my kids were coping.

I knew he would. I used to pour my heart out to 'Dubes' when I was going through my worst times and he would listen and advise like a good friend.

What I didn't know until later was that he was having plenty of personal problems of his own and yet he never mentioned them. That, to me, was the sign of a true friend.

He refused to unburden himself because he was intent on seeing me through my troubles first.

'Dubes' was the one friend I asked to come and see me in prison towards the end of my stay. He gets me totally.

He was there for me the night before I went to court for sentencing, while I was in prison and when I came out. His loyalty never wavered.

We're both strong-minded, opinionated individuals but most of all we respect each other. We sometimes agree to disagree, but all in all to me he is the true definition of a close friend.

When I first signed for Crystal Palace, Bruce Dyer was there. He was Britain's first million-pound teenage footballer after moving from Watford to Selhurst Park and we just clicked straight away. We had the same interests in music, in going out and we both became born-again Christians, although Bruce has never lost his faith like I did.

We were both party animals back in the day. He was earning good money for that era and he liked to spend it on having a good time. He fancied himself as a DJ and he became a very good one.

Footballers don't tend to make many friends in the game during their career, but me and Bruce have stuck together for 15 years.

He's matured a lot now and he runs football schools in Barnsley where he finished his career. He's still heavily involved in church and charity work so he's a busy man, but he has always got time for me.

He wrote to me in prison and he was in touch as soon as I came out. It takes a special friend to be there when you mess up and people like Bruce and 'Dubes' would be the same with me whether I lived in a mansion or a cardboard box.

Millions will know MC Harvey of So Solid Crew fame. I know him as Michael Harvey, one of my closest friends of the last few years. Harvey was a decent footballer. He was a left-winger at Chelsea when I was at Palace and he was a decent player.

Harvey could have joined me at Palace and he often wished he had because he was lost at Chelsea who had too many talented kids for him to get past and into the senior squad.

I admire Harvey as he didn't let the fact that his football didn't take off bother him. He dedicated himself to another field.

He didn't do too bad either racking up 4 million in album sales, but he was at the ground on my Palace debut and he's still there for me now, giving me plenty of help as I try and make a career in music myself.

He's not doing that just as a mate though. He listened to the tracks that I sent him because of our friendship, but the fact that he performed on my own song 'Finally' was proof that he thought I had some ability.

We speak regularly. Getting him to come on a dinner date is impossible though, like finding Father Christmas, as London men don't like to leave London, certainly not for places like Peterborough and Northampton!

But we have open conversations all the time though. He told me once that he'd been through some hard times over the last four years.

We set up a little label, M & L recordings, and he helps me with the distribution of my music.

His heart sank though when I told him I might go down for some petty motoring offences. It broke my heart as well as I was supposed to be going on the Tim Westwood show on Radio One to discuss my music, but when the BBC found out that I might go to prison they cancelled me.

It was yet another example of the stupid police and CPS action against me, fucking me over and I was paying for it yet again.

'Finally' was even released when I was inside, on my mum's birthday, which was hard for me, but it's doing well and been downloaded several thousand times.

Harvey could have cut me off when I went inside as he might not have wanted to be associated with someone in my situation. It could have caused him a headache as we'd just collaborated on a song, but he was too genuine a person for that, he was too real.

He was with me at my house the night before sentencing and with me at court.

I met Jason Lee at Peterborough. He told me that the first day I walked into the dressing room that he reckoned I was full of myself, I really fancied myself. He wasn't wrong.

He soon realised that I could back my attitude up with performances. We got on well on the field and we became great friends off it.

Jason was best man at my wedding to Sofia. He wrote to me in prison and he was a massive help when I was having problems with Vanessa, my first wife.

I walked out on Vanessa once and Jason put me up in his house in Nottingham. He and his wife Ann were just brilliant with me. They had four kids, but made room for me.

Mind you when I was woken at 1am by Ann telling me that Vanessa had turned up outside the house, I realised I'd probably overstayed my welcome and I went back home!

It was an act of kindness from Jason and his family that I've never forgotten though.

DJ Spoony is one of the most intelligent men I know. I met him through Bruce Dyer who liked to do a bit of DJ-ing himself.

'Spoons' was the celebrity DJ of the UK Garage scene and he was just very good at what he did. He also loved his football so he found it easy to befriend a lot of the players especially as our industries regularly crossed.

Me and Bruce went to alot of the raves 'Spoons' attended and we had a cracking holiday in Tenerife once and stayed in touch afterwards.

'Spoons' reached out to me when I was in prison as well which was just a great gesture from him.

I met Zephaniah Anderson through the church. He was a very, very close friend, who I lost contact with for a little while.

If ever I needed any help with understanding the scriptures,

Zephaniah was the man. He never forced his beliefs on me, but he could articulate things so well and with such clarity I still turn to him whenever I'm struggling to understand life.

We are back in touch now and he co-wrote my song 'Give it To Me'. He's a very blessed individual and a fantastic graphic designer.

I did an article in the Daily Mail once detailing my depression and revealing my suicide bid.

After the article was published Darren Byfield was the first footballer to reach out to me and apologise for not realising how down I was at that time. He was brilliant, genuine and offered me help with anything I needed.

I didn't get many calls from other footballers. Clinton Morrison got in touch as did a couple of Peterborough players, Simon Rea and Adam Newton.

I also have to mention Marcus Hall who was another ex-team-mate to write to me. We used to room together when we were at Coventry and we shared many laughs at each other's expense.

We played together at Northampton as well. His dad, who was a big fan of mine, sadly passed away and I went to the funeral. I was in a lonely place myself then so I felt very sad for my friend.

I can't imagine how I would feel if I lost my dad. I love Marcus to bits, he is the perfect man in my eyes and he has a beautiful family himself.

Well-known sprinter Darren Campbell is another friend I respect greatly. I only met him through chance quite recently, but he has also worked himself back up to achieve great things after overcoming some serious challenges and that automatically gives us a connection. He's simply a winner.

Andrew Harvey, the kitman at Coventry, is another man I want to thank. He was always on my side no matter what was going on. I'm still in touch with the school friends who have never judged me like Darren Doyley and Desmond Senior.

They run a barbers shop together in Thornton Heath. Desmond was a decent footballer at Palace himself.

The biggest compliment that I can pay to my boys from the place where I grew up is that when we took different paths and they realised I was chasing a football career they gave me their blessings. When I became successful they showed me love and I never forgot that. I once went to their barbers shop and gave them a man of the match champagne bottle that I'd won the previous weekend.

And when I hit hard times, they treated me just the same. They never stopped being solid, loyal friends no matter what circumstances we were all experiencing.

David Maddy, Mark Petty and Ales Trew are other old school pals who deserve a mention. They provided some great memories from my younger days.

We'd all go to a jazz night club on a Wednesday night in Purley Way and hold our own dance competitions.

We'd form a massive circle and take it in turns to get in the middle of the dance floor and strut our stuff. I had some moves and I was a regular winner. The girls certainly loved a good dancer, happy days!

And finally, I thank everyone who sent me messages on Twitter while I was serving time. You know who you are and I wish I could write all the names on this page, but I received so many it would be impossible.

But thanks for your love and support anyway.

Also thanks to the ones that should have supported me and wrote to me but didn't. I'm glad now as it makes things a lot clearer about what and who is important in my life.

I made mistakes and I still make them. I'm not perfect, but one thing I do know is my heart and having the right people and family around you will only make it stronger.